A Tailoring Manual

THE MACMILLAN COMPANY
NEW YORK · CHICAGO
DALLAS · ATLANTA · SAN FRANCISCO
LONDON · MANILA

THE MACMILLAN COMPANY
OF CANADA, LIMITED
TORONTO

A Tailoring Manual

GERTRUDE STRICKLAND

Professor Emeritus
Clothing, Textiles, and Related Arts
Oregon State College
Corvallis, Oregon

THE MACMILLAN COMPANY New York

Foreword

Accuracy in tailoring details is absolutely essential in securing a well-made garment. Short cuts will hinder the achievement of such a goal. Much of the work involved in a tailored garment is hidden from the eye, but it is important. Sufficient time should be allowed for the construction of a tailored garment, for it cannot be made as quickly as a dress. Accuracy in detail, frequent comparison between the two sides, and careful workmanship will be justified, for the finished garment quickly shows up any carelessness.

The following instructions are planned in sequence in so far as is possible, to guide the home sewer in the construction of a suit, a coat, or slacks. Not all instructions in basic sewing can be included in this manual, since there are adequate texts already available. This manual, with its illustrations, should assist one in developing better constructions in tailoring, give one an appreciation of what goes into a custom-made garment, and aid one in the selection of future ready-made suits, coats, and slacks.

G. S.

v

Table of Contents

Foreword   v
Glossary of Terms   1
Selection of Fabric and Findings for Garment   3
   Fabrics of Wool or Worsted   3
   Materials Used in the Making of Suit or Coat   4
Shrinking   5
Laboratory Equipment and Tools   6
   Directions for Making Laboratory Equipment   6
Adhesive Paper Dress Form   9
Measurements   14
   Preparation for Measurements   14
   Measurement Sheets   16
   Measurement Sheet for Raglan Sleeve   17
Measuring the Commercial Pattern   18
   Suggested Allowances for Ease   20
   Variances in Commercial Patterns   21
   Grading Patterns   21
Pattern Alteration   25
   Darts (Four Main Positions)   25
   Other Dart Positions Used in Garment Construction 26
   Enlarged Bust Alteration   28
   Round Shoulder Alteration   30
   Widen Shoulders   31
   Narrow Shoulders   31
   Types of Set-in Sleeves Used in Tailored Garments 32
   Sleeve Cap Increase in Height   32
   Sleeve Cap Increase of Sleeve with Seam at Center 33
   Sleeve Cap Increase for a Two-piece Sleeve   35
Making the Muslin Garment   37
   Cutting the Muslin Jacket   37
   Suggested Allowances for Finished Seams and Hems 38
   Marking the Garment   38
   Basting the Jacket   38
   Fitting the Jacket or Coat   39
   Self Fitting   39
   Shoulder Pads   40
   Figure Problems   41
   Garment Problems in Fitting   41
   Baste Collar to Muslin Jacket   50
   Preparing the Sleeve for Fitting   50
   Fitting the Sleeves into the Armscye   50

Basting the Sleeve into the Armscye 51
Marking the Fitted Muslin 54
General Suggestions in Garment Construction 55
Cutting the Wool Garment 56
Planning the Wool Garment Layout for Cutting 56
Lining 56
Interlining 57
Canvas (or Interfacings) 57
Stay Line Stitching Before Basting 59
Steaming Wool 60
Making the Skirt 62
Basting the Skirt 62
Fitting the Skirt 63
Belts 63
Fitting Problems in Skirt 64
Rebasting the Skirt 65
Directions for Stitching Darts and Seams 66
Outside Stitching on Pleats 66
Zipper Placket 67
Fastening the Belt to the Skirt 69
Snaps, Hooks and Eyes 69
Marking the Hem of the Skirt 70
Shrinking Hem Turn-up 70
Hem Finishes 70
Pleated Skirt 72
Inside Seam Finishes 74
Seam Finishes on Right Side of Garment 74
Fasteners on Garments 77
Corded Buttonhole 78
Piped Buttonholes 78
Buttonhole Facing 80
Worked Buttonhole 82
Buttonhole Loops 82
Sewing on Garment Fastenings 83
Double-Breasted Garments 84
Making the Jacket or Coat 85
Preparing Inside Cuts on Garment Surface 85
Basting the Garment 86
Fitting the Wool Garment 86
Stitching and Steaming Darts and Seams 86
Basting the Lining 86
Lining Shield Pattern 86
Stitching the Canvas Darts and Seams 87
Basting the Canvas to the Garment 87
Pad Stitching the Garment Fronts 88
Taping the Garment Fronts 89
Steaming the Two Fronts after Taping 91
Taping Underarm of Armscye 91
Pull-up Stitch 92
Attaching Facing to the Garment 92
Fly Facing 92
Grading Seams at Edge of Garment 94

Curved Edges   95
Stitching Shoulder Seams   95
Pockets   96
Welt Pocket   96
Flap Pocket   99
Corded Pocket   100
Patch Pocket   102
Simulated Patch Pocket   103
Saddlebag Pocket   104
Pocket in a Seam   105
Pocket Made in the Design Line of a Garment   107
Pocket Between Lining and Facing of Garment   108
Decorative Tacks   109
Collar   111
Making the Collar   111
Join Collar to Garment   113
Shawl Collar   114
Taping the Shawl Collar   115
Facing the Shawl Collar   115
Collarless Garments   117
Sleeves   118
Fitting Sleeves into the Wool Garment   118
Stitching the Sleeves   118
Marking Hems of the Sleeves and Jacket   119
Mitered Corner   119
Sleeve Finishes at Wrist   120
Bias for Binding   121
Bound Edge   122
Fitted or Shaped Facing   122
Fastening Shoulder Pads to Garment   122
Hemming the Jacket or Coat   123
Hemming the Jacket   123
Hemming the Long Coat   124
Basting the Garment Facing into Place   124
Lining the Garment   126
Lining the Body of the Garment with Set-in Sleeves   126
Lining the Sleeve   128
Lining the Vent and the Bottom of the Long Coat   129
Hemming the Lining of the Long Coat   130
Interlining   131
Unlined Garment   132
Lining the Raglan or Kimono Garment   132
French Tacks   133
Edge Stitching the Garment   134
Arm Straps for Coats   136
Slacks   137
Pockets   141
Finishing Waistline of Slacks   144
Cuffs on Slacks   145
Plain Hem at Bottom of Slacks   145
Final Steaming   148

A Tailoring Manual

Glossary of Terms

Armscye or Armhole: The garment edge that fits around the arm at the shoulder end.

Basting: Long stitches used to hold garment edges together for fitting or stitching.

Bias: A diagonal line of seam, cut or stitched across a fabric.
- a. True bias: True bias for cutting bias bands or portions of a garment is found by folding the fabric so that the warp thread parallels the filling thread. The fold thus formed is a true bias.
- b. Garment bias: Any bias not a true bias is called a garment bias, such as a side seam of a skirt.

Break line: The folded edge of a lapel.

Bridle stay or tape: A stay tape along the lapel fold to prevent stretching, also to help insure the fit of the bust of the garment.

Buttonhole twist: A strong silk thread used for working buttonholes, French tacks, and belt loops.

Catstitch or catch stitch: A method of hemming the raw edge to garment by taking a tiny stitch in the fabric parallel to the hem, then cross the cut edge and take a stitch in the hem edge. These stitches are ¼ inch apart and ¼ inch between the two rows. The direction of stitching is left to right, the stitches cross and resemble a herringbone stitch.

Canvas: Fabric used as inner stiffening on a tailored garment to give it body and shape.
- a. Wigan: Cotton muslin in varying degrees of stiffness.
- b. Hymo: A wiry canvas used for padding or stiffening.
- c. Haircloth or horsehair: Stiff, wiry fabric made of cotton, worsted, or linen warp, with a filling of horsehair.
- d. Linen: Stiff linen canvas for stiffening.

Chalk: A waxed or dry square of chalk used for marking.

Collar stand: The folded edge of a collar of a jacket or suit.

Dart: Short tapering seam used in a garment to insure a better fit.

Ease thread: A fine running or gathering thread used along the stitching line, where that edge will be matched to a shorter space.

Flap: Finished fold of material hanging over the top of a pocket.

Fly facing: A closing in a garment so constructed that it conceals the fastenings.

Godet: A piece of fabric shaped like a section of pie, inserted into a garment edge to add ease or fullness.

Gore: A section or panel of a skirt.

Grading: The art of increasing or decreasing a pattern from one size to another.

Grading seams: Cutting one seam edge slightly narrower than its matching seam to decrease bulk at the edge of garment.

Grosgrain: A firm, stiff ribbon or fabric made with crosswise ribs.

Gusset: A shaped section at underarm of garment to allow more ease and strength.

Haircloth: See canvas.

1

Ham cushion: An egg-shaped, hard-stuffed cushion used to press shaped portions of a garment.

Hymo: See canvas.

Interlining: Cotton flannel or wool used between lining and garment to add warmth.

Lapel: A reverse and collar at garment front.

Linen: See canvas.

Manila tag: A thin crisp cardboard 30″ by 24″, 125-pound weight. (Referred to in text as Tag.)

Nap: Pile of a fabric.

Notch lapel: A lapel with a **V**-shaped break in it.

Pad stitch: A small prick-stitch used to fasten canvas to the wrong side of the lapel or collar of a garment to give it shape. It is made by sticking the needle through the canvas, picking up a few yarns on the back surface of the wool, and bringing needle up to the right side of the canvas. Stitches zig-zag, the spread is ¼ inch, and stitches are ¼ inch apart. Threads at stitch point do not cross.

Paddle or beater: A hardwood paddle or rectangular block used to pound thick edges or buttonholes to flatten them when steaming.

Pick stitch: A hand stitch in place of machine stitch used around edges on tailored garments.

Plumb line: A string with a weight attached at the end, which is used against a seam to determine its straightness.

Purl: A fine loop made along the worked buttonhole edge.

Reversible: A garment so constructed that it looks equally well with either side exposed.

Saddle stitch: A decorative hand stitch using coarse thread and long stitches, usually along the edge of a garment.

Silesia: A twill cotton fabric used in pockets, linings, and facings in slacks and men's tailored garments.

Sleeve cap: The section above a line drawn across a sleeve from armpit to armpit.

Stab stitch: A stitch made by pushing the needle straight through thicknesses of material, pulling the thread after, then returning the needle and thread in the same manner.

Stay stitch: A temporary machine stitch along a stitching edge to hold it in place until permanent stitch is used.

Stiletto: A short, slender pointed instrument for making eyelet holes.

Sunbak: A trade-mark for patented satin lining with wool backing. Use of this lining eliminates the handling of extra interlining.

Tailor tacks: A method of transferring pattern markings onto a cut garment, using short looped stitches through two thicknesses of fabric. When fabric is separated and looped stitches cut, the two sections are marked identically. If darning cotton is used to tailor tack, only one stitch is used through the two thicknesses as it does not slip out as readily as sewing cotton.

Tailor's square: A ruler with a right-angle turn.

Vent: A lapped opening from the bottom edge of a garment.

Wadding: A prepared sheet of carded cotton used for padding.

Warp: The lengthwise thread of a fabric.

Wigan: See canvas.

Woof: The crosswise or filling thread of a fabric.

Selection of Fabric and Findings for Garment

Care should be used in the selection of fabric, and one should purchase the best woolen or worsted material with the money available.

The use of the garment must be considered, whether for utility or dressy occasional wear. Many hard twills become shiny with use and are not practical for utility purposes. Also twills are more difficult to tailor because they do not shrink so easily as tweeds and are more likely to show any poor workmanship.

The selection of color will depend upon one's present wardrobe, the accessories on hand, and one's preference for color. A conservative color is usually more practical because it may be worn longer without going out of style, or one's becoming tired of it.

The lining should be purchased along with the fabric. It should be durable in a matching, neutral, or contrasting color of pure-dye satin, silk, crepe, or taffeta; or acetate and rayon satin, crepe, or twill; milium satin or crepe fabric with metallic backing; or Sunbak, a satin fabric with a wool backing.

Matching or contrasting colored buttons may be purchased; or buttons may be made from the fabric of the garment.

The selection of a pattern is important. Lines should be flattering to the figure and suitable for the fabric selected. One should get the correct size as nearly as is possible in order to eliminate alteration problems.

FABRICS OF WOOL OR WORSTED

Astrakhan: Pile fabric resembling Persian lamb. Coats.

Bedford cord: Corded material of woolen or worsted with woven vertical rib. Excellent wearing quality, unless weave is loose. Suitable for slacks, sportwear, or coats.

Bengaline: Rib weave similar to poplin. For coats or suits.

Bouclé: Yarns with loops which give fabric a rough appearance. Suits or coats.

Broadcloth: Rich-looking fabric with a nap lying in one direction. Smooth surface. Suits or coats.

Cashmere: Woolen suiting with smooth surface or nap. Twill or plain weave. Suits or slacks.

Camel's hair: Twilled and napped fabric in neutral or dyed colors. Coats.

Cheviot: Rough-surfaced fabric with twill weave. Suits or coats.

Covert cloth: Twilled fabric with mottled effect due to the use of two-ply warp yarn of white and color. Suits, coats, or slacks.

Crepe: Fine crepe spiral-twisted worsted with tone on tone. Light weight. Suits.

Duvetyn: Suede-surfaced effect with cotton back. Suits or coats. Not durable.

Flannel: Soft-napped surface with plain or twill weave. Suits or slacks.

French serge: Smooth firm fabric, twill weave. Suits, slacks, or summer coats. Becomes shiny very quickly.

Gabardine: Smooth, hard-surfaced twill fabric which is soft and dull. Suits, slacks, or summer coats.

Homespun: Loose plain weave and rough in texture. Suits, coats.

Poplin: Corded effect. Plain weave. Suits.

Ratiné: Loosely woven, nubby, plain weave. Suits or coats.

Serge: Worsted fabric, twill weave, not as fine or soft as French serge. Wears shiny. Suits, slacks, or summer coats.

Sharkskin: A firm fabric of plain or basket weave. Suits, slacks.

Tweed: Rough-surfaced in plain or twill weave in light or heavy weight. Suits, slacks, or coats.

Whipcord: Woolen or worsted twill. Slacks, suits.

MATERIALS USED IN THE MAKING OF SUIT OR COAT

1. Wool fabric cut along the grain (either torn or cut along a pulled thread.)

Allow 6 inches in a garment length for shrinkage and for extra seam allowance.

A garment cut on the bias, or one with a pleated skirt or a flared coat will need 12 inches, since more yardage is required in cutting. A medium or large plaid will need at least 18 inches for shrinking and *waste* in cutting since all plaids *must* be matched.

Allow extra length for the tall figure because yardage estimations are for those of average height.

2. Lining cut along grain. Allow the same amount as for the wool for extra height.

3. Canvas with ends torn or cut along grain. Use any one of the following:

 a. Wigan or soft unbleached muslin: a very soft material suitable for soft dressmaker suit. Used across upper back in nearly all garments.

 b. Hymo: best weight for most tailored garments.

 c. Haircloth or horsehair: very stiff and wiry.

 d. Tailor's linen: may be used instead of hymo, but it wrinkles while being handled.

4. Shoulder pads may be purchased ready-made or made at home.

5. Linen tape for taping garment edges. Rayon tape, straight, may be used for very soft or thin fabric.

6. Interlining (optional): Cotton flannel or wool interlining.

7. Lead weights for jacket hem.

8. Zipper for skirt.

9. Sewing silk: 4 or 5 spools for stitching.

10. Matching mercerized cotton thread for some hand work on inside of garment.

11. Buttonhole twist for tacks, buttonholes, if worked, and for sewing on buttons.

12. Heavy-duty thread in contrasting color for basting.

13. Darning cotton for tailor's tacks.

14. Hooks and eyes for skirt belt.

15. Grosgrain ribbon for skirt belt.

Shrinking

All wool fabrics, whether labeled preshrunk or not, should be shrunk before being made into a garment. Each end of fabric *must* be torn or cut along the thread before shrinking to save loss of yardage. This may be suggested to the clerk when purchasing fabric.

Wet one half of a sheet and wring out; then fold the dry end into the wet end and wring again until the sheet is evenly damp all over.

Smooth out the sheet on cutting table.

Lay the folded wool along the edge of wet sheet and fold the remaining sheet width over the top of the wool.

Loosely fold the sheet and wool together and allow to stand at least six hours, preferably overnight.

Remove wool from sheet, and while damp pull it diagonally into shape until the folded edges and ends of wool lie square with the table.

Loosely woven woolens will not need to be pressed and may be left to dry on table.

Smooth, closely woven woolens will need pressing. Place on broad pressing table with fabric squared to edges.

With warm iron press lightly with the length grain, but not over the center fold as this causes a sharp crease.

Turn material over and press second side.

Open up fabric and press along crease.

After being pressed, the fabric will still be slightly damp; spread it smoothly on cutting table to dry thoroughly, having both cross and length grains parallel to table edges.

Canvas, linen tape, grosgrain belting:

To shrink canvas, fold the material loosely back and forth like an accordion and submerge into container of hot water, allowing to stand until cold.

Remove from water bath, strip water out by hand, roll in cloth or spread smoothly on flat surface to dry partially before ironing.

Do not wring out the materials from water bath; this causes wrinkles which are difficult to iron out.

Keep the grain of material parallel with table edges while ironing.

To prevent the filling in canvas from adhering to the iron, place a piece of tissue or thin wrapping paper over the wet canvas while ironing.

Linen tape and grosgrain belting may be placed in the same water bath with the canvas and stripped through the fingers to remove excess water. When partially dry, press parallel to a yardstick to prevent curves in the tape.

Laboratory Equipment and Tools

Cutting table
Sewing machine
Pressing equipment
  Sleeve board
  Seam board
  Press cloth of drilling or its equivalent
  Press cloth of cheesecloth
  Velvet board and cleaner brush
  Hardwood paddle
  Iron
    Plain
    Steam
  Tailor's press pads, large and small
  Sheet for shrinking, 4 to 4½ yards long
  Turkish towel, heavy, white
  Tag board strips, 2 or 3 inches wide, any length
    needed, or heavy wrapping paper if tag is
    not available
Shears, 7½ or 8 inches
Pinking shears
Buttonhole cutter
Transfer paper, light and dark
Tracing wheel
Tailor's chalk, wax and dry
Yardstick
Square
Skirt marker
Full-length mirror
Dress form
Needles, sizes 7 to 10
Thimble
Pins
Heavy-duty basting thread in color
Silk thread for stitching garment

Buttonhole twist
Darning cotton for tailor's tacks
Tape line
Pencil
Stiletto
Bodkin
Edge marker or short rule
Seam gauge
Tailor-trik—a patented wooden pointed tool for
  turning and spreading points
Plumb line

The above equipment will be used in a tailoring class, but for home tailoring one may improvise and get good results with less equipment.

DIRECTIONS FOR MAKING LABORATORY EQUIPMENT

Figure 1.

Some laboratory equipment may be made at home and will afford great convenience for doing home sewing. The dimensions given below are approximate measurements. The materials used in seam board, sleeve board, paddle, and sawdust for pads should be of hardwood to eliminate any possibility of pitch appearing.

Dimensions for the following equipment are listed on the drawings in Figure 1, *a* through *i*.

  a. Press pads: These are made of sturdy duck or similar material. Cut two oval pieces and stitch together with a 2-inch boxing, leaving a 4-inch opening along one seam at one end. Stuff tightly with hardwood sawdust, then sew opening securely.

    This pad is used to steam any part of the

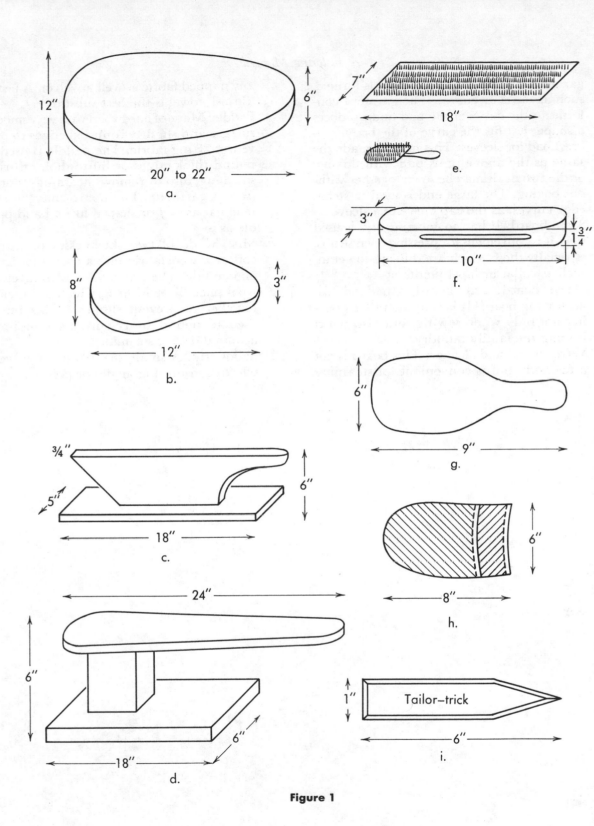

Figure 1

garment where a shaped surface is formed, such as darts or curves. The garment conforms to the curve of the pad and produces a shape that fits the curve of the body.

b. Press pad for sleeves: This may be made the same as the above press pad with boxing, or the two ovals may be sewn together without boxing. The large end is used to steam edge curves, as the cap curve of a sleeve.

c. Seam board: It has no covering and is used raw. It is convenient for pressing open seams, especially those which are difficult to get at, such as collar or lapel points.

d. Sleeve board: This board is padded like an ironing board. It is convenient for pressing not only when sewing, but also when ironing the family laundry.

e. Velvet board and cleaner: This board is not a necessity but is convenient for steaming any napped fabric as well as velvet. A heavy Turkish towel is the best substitute.

f, g. Paddle: Made of hardwood with very smooth surface and slightly rounded edges to prevent marring fabric. The paddle is used to pound thick edges or buttonholes during steaming, also to remove steaming "shine" from a garment. The board may be rectangular as in *f* or shaped like a hand paddle as in *g*.

h. Mit: Made of two thicknesses of sturdy cotton or wool fabric with a pocket for hand on one side. The mit is filled with layers of wool piled ¾ inch thick, which are tacked together to prevent slipping. This mit is used to pound shiny surfaces sometimes acquired during steaming.

i. Tailor-trik: A small, inexpensive tool very effective in turning angles or points.

Adhesive Paper Dress Form

Because it is difficult for a person to fit herself, and a fitter is not always available, a dress form the exact duplicate of one's figure is almost essential. One that is made on the individual is more satisfactory and less expensive than the commercially made form. For that reason, the instructions for making a form have been included in this tailoring manual.

Figure 2.

Materials needed:

1. Two shirts of thin knit material such as **T** shirts. Thin muslin cut on the bias and about 5 inches wide, to build up a neckline; or gauze tubing shaped to the figure; or a packaged dress form kit (from a department store) which will contain all necessary material.
2. Two rolls of medium weight adhesive paper, one inch wide.
3. Eight yards of colored scotch tape, ¼ inch wide.
4. Stiff, corrugated cardboard, large enough to cut out a base for the largest hip size, and a neck size piece.
5. Other materials: two sponges, two small basins for water, needle, thread, sharp scissors, surgical scissors if available, pencil, yardstick, rule, tapeline, sharp razor blade with one cutting edge only, shellac, small paint brush.

Method of procedure:

Four persons are necessary to construct the form quickly; two to moisten strips, and two to paste strips to person, one working on the front and one on the back. Allow one hour for making the form on the figure and one hour for finishing it after it is removed from the figure.

The person should wear a bra and girdle which give desirable style lines. She should stand so that her hands may be placed on the back of a chair or rest on the edge of a table for support.

To cut the paper, hold the roll with edge extending over a table edge, and cut through the roll with a razor blade.

All strips should be cut before starting to make the form on the person.

Keep separate on table each group of strips cut from the two rolls of tape to prevent confusion and to speed up the operation.

a. Diagram showing the depth each group of strips is cut from the two rolls. Each group should be labeled as it is cut.
1. First group of strips is cut ¾ inch in from outside of both rolls and are approximately 15 to 12 inches long. These strips are used from shoulder to waist on first layer, and diagonally from neck down front and back on the second layer.
2. Second group of strips, around 12 to 9 inches, is cut ¾ inch from outside of each roll. These strips are used on the first layer from waist to lower hip edge, and

on the second layer down from the neck in front and back.

3. Third group of strips, around 9 to 5 inches, cut ¾ inch in from outside edge of roll.

   These strips are used diagonally under the arm on both first and second layers in making the form.

4. Cut around 250 3-inch strips for finishing edges of form and for joining the two sections.

b. Put the shirt, or substitute, on the person and sew edges together so that the shirt fits smoothly and firmly on the figure. It should run up onto the neck to form a neckband, extend out over upper arm to form a smooth armscye, and extend well below the widest hips. Pull the shirt down smoothly from shoulder, and paste a long strip of moistened tape closely around the normal waistline, overlapping tape ends to prevent slipping. Paste another strip of tape closely below the widest hip. Paste strips curving under each bust to preserve contour.

c. First layer of strips, 12 to 15 inches. Begin at center front and back, paste moistened strips on the figure from neck and shoulder edges to taped waistline, overlapping strips ¾ of the strip width. Let strips curve to body contour as they will, and if too long tear off excess length.

   Continue pasting strips to armscye edge, overlapping strips at top of shoulder. Repeat for second side of front and back. From waist to lower hip edge, paste 9- to 12-inch strips at right angles to waist, joining tape ends to those above the waist. Paste short 5- to 9-inch strips diagonally from underarm to lower hip edge, allowing strips to overlap front and back strips at side front and back. Repeat for second side.

d. Second layer of tape. Above the waist use 9- to 12-inch strips. Start just below the neck, paste strips diagonally across front, alternating strips from right and left side, having strips overlap at top of shoulder.

   As you continue downward, the ends of strips should touch and form the upper armscye. Continue these crossed strips down the body to the lower hip line edge, using 12- to 15-inch strips below the waistline. This should form a smooth surface over the entire figure, especially at the waist where

joinings had occured on the first layer. The second layer from underarm to lower hip line is reinforced with 5- to 9-inch strips the same as in *c*, the first layer.

e. Reinforce around armscye to form a good shape, using 3- to 5-inch strips. Some persons may wish a short sleeve cap. This is formed from 1 to 3 inches beyond armscye at shoulder tip, using short 3- to 5-inch strips, building a smooth upper arm curve, allowing strips to follow the arm curve when pasting on. (It is difficult to put on and remove garments with an extended sleeve cap.)

   Finish the neck with one layer of 6- to 9-inch strips around the neck to form a good shape until dress form is removed from person. The neck can be reinforced more sturdily when form is removed.

f. Measure and mark the form before removing.

	Form	*Person*	*Differences*
Neck			
Bust			
Waist			
Widest hip			

   Measure from floor up to within 2 or 3 inches below the widest hip and carefully mark for the base of the form.

g. Mark for removing form from person, down center front and back with ruled line, across front and back at intervals for matching when joining half sections. To remove form from the figure, cut with a one-edged razor blade down center front and back marked lines. Be careful to cut through paper only. Finish cutting through the fabric with surgical scissors or sharp-pointed shears.

   Remove the two sections.

   Either before the form is made or after it is removed, measure the person at the following positions and record in *f:* neck, bust, waist, and widest hip.

   Compute the difference between the person and the form at neck, bust, waist, and hip. Divide by 4 and remove this difference from the two center-front and two center-back edges of form.

   Cut smoothly along marked hipline which is parallel to the floor.

a.

b.

c.

d.

e.

f.

Figure 2

11

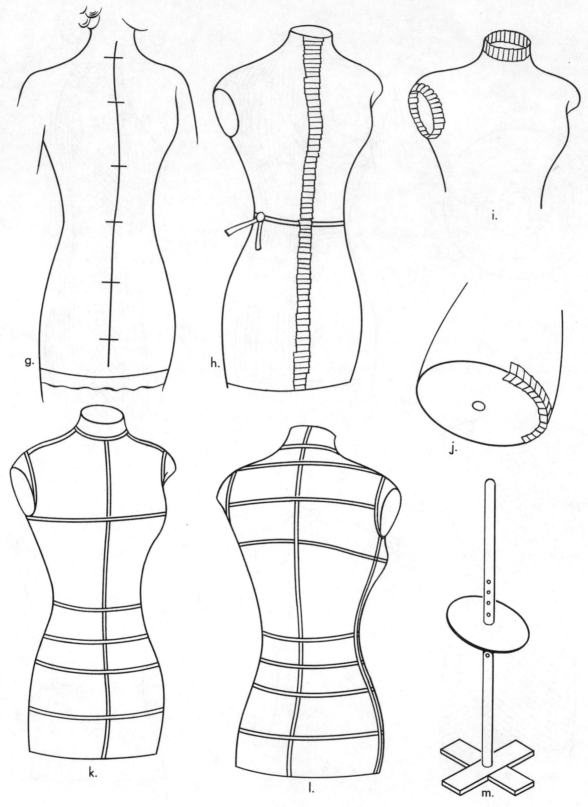

g.

h.

i.

j.

k.

l.

m.

Figure 2 (Continued)

12

Hold each section up to the light; and reinforce on the inside of the form any spots that seem thin.

h. Join sections, using 3-inch strips.

Place fronts down on the table with edges and cross markings matching both front and back, and pin a tape securely around the waist.

Paste 3-inch strips across cut edges of front, first on the outside and then on the inside.

These strips should be closely overlapped to hold edges permanently. Repeat for back.

i. Trim neck and armscye edges smoothly and reinforce with 3-inch strips around cut edge.

Trim bottom of form along marked line until it stands evenly on the table.

j. Place bottom of form on paper and mark around the hips, also mark center front and center back.

Repeat the same for the neck.

Cut cardboard from paper patterns and cut a 1¼-inch hole in the center of each.

Fit the cardboard flush into the inside edges of the hip and neck and join to the form with 3-inch strips.

k, l. Outer Covering. To keep the paper edges from curling, the form should be shellacked and thoroughly dried.

A top shirt is tightly and smoothly fitted over form, sewing where necessary, and taping at armscye, neck and under the lower edge of the form.

Using ¼-inch colored tape, mark the following measurement positions: center front, center back, neck, shoulder width, back width, bust, waist, armscye, 3-inch hip, 6-inch hip, widest hip.

m. Standard. A standard is needed in order to use the form successfully. This is made, using two 2″ x 4″ x 18″ pieces of wood for base, and a pole 5 to 5½ feet tall and 1¼ inch in diameter with nail holes bored up the length to adjust the height.

An oval board cut from plywood should be smaller than the base of the form. Bore a 1½-inch hole in the center. This oval is slipped on the pole to rest over a large nail and support the form.

Measurements

PREPARATION FOR MEASUREMENTS

The measurements for a garment should be taken over smooth-fitting undergarments with dress removed. If a heavy garment is worn underneath the jacket or coat, additional measurements should be taken over that garment so as to estimate the added increase. It is difficult for one to measure herself. A well-fitted garment in the wardrobe may be measured for size, or the pattern may be pinned together and held against the figure for size. The last two methods are not too accurate.

Accurate measurements for both the figure and the pattern used are needed for all garment construction. The differences in the two measurements should be compared and listed on the measurement sheet in the space allowed, or upon the pattern itself at the point where the variances occur.

The fullness for ease that is allowed on the garment will depend upon the type of garment being constructed, the type of individual figure, the weight and type of fabric used, the purpose for which the garment is intended, the prevailing fashion, and the individual's preference for the tightness or looseness of the garment.

The suggested ease allowance in Column 2 on the measurement sheet is for minimum amounts and is to be used as a guide in planning each garment made.

While measuring the figure, observe any figure variances and list them on measurement sheet. When checking the pattern, one can make the necessary alterations.

It is much easier to take accurate measurements if the figure is carefully marked with a soft pencil at important points between which measurements are to be taken.

The following figures and instructions offer a guide for marking the figure.

Figure 3.

a, b	Fasten tape snugly around the normal waistline. Use a beaded chain or string to locate positions on the figure to be marked. The chain (secured in a hardware store) is more accurate and easier to handle than a string.
1	Center front neck
2, 2′	Sides of neck
	Place chain closely around the base of the neck, touching the prominent bone at back neck and just above the two bones at throat hollow at front.
3	Center back neck
	Place the chain or string around the armscye, perpendicular to the floor, and mark.
4	Highest point on shoulders
5, 5′	Swing the chain or string outward ½ to ¾ inches from 4 for the correct shoulder tip.
6, 6′	Locate width of chest, 6, 6′, halfway between shoulder tip, 5, 5′, and a point opposite the underarm.
7, 7′	Locate width of back, halfway between shoulder tip and a point opposite the underarm.

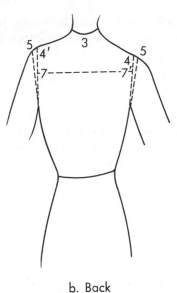

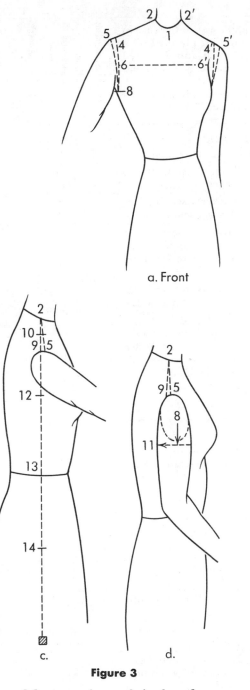

a. Front

b. Back

c.　　　　　　d.

Figure 3

8　　Measure down 2 inches from armpit and mark.

c, d　To mark normal shoulder line on *c*, stand at the side of the person being measured and place the chain or string from 2 to 5 along top of shoulder. At Point 5 on *c* swing the chain ½ inch toward the back and mark 9.

2, 9　Average normal shoulder line of the figure.

10　　Point halfway between 2 and 9. The shoulder dart starts from this point.

8　　At Position 8 on Figure *d,* place the chain or string around the arm (with arm relaxed) parallel to the floor and mark 11 on outer arm.

11　　Indicates the base of the sleeve cap from which the sleeve cap height is obtained.

9, 11　Indicates the sleeve cap height plus ½ inch for ease at sleeve top, plus ½ to 1 inch for shoulder pads, if used, depending on the thickness of the pads. The three combined measurements give the correct height of sleeve cap.

Underarm seam:

To locate the normal underarm seam, stand at the side of a person, place a plumb line (a string with a weight at one end) at Point 9 on *c* at tip of shoulder seam, and allow the weight to drop free. With the arm hugging the body, swing the arm forward and press the string against the figure under the arm and mark with pins parallel to string:

12　Bust line
13　Waist line
14　Widest hip position

Marking the figure with pencil and drawing a tape around waistline will help eliminate much of the guesswork involved in trying to find correct positions on the body. Following the directions on the measurement sheet on the following pages should result in accurate measurements of the figure.

MEASUREMENT SHEETS

Figure 4 a.

Note: The same lettering used in Figure 3 when marking the figure with pencil is not used in Figure 4 when taking actual measurements, as the markings on the figure were used only to make figure measurements more accurate.

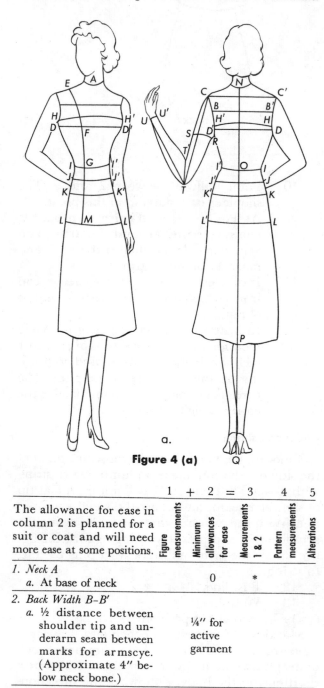

a.

Figure 4 (a)

The allowance for ease in column 2 is planned for a suit or coat and will need more ease at some positions.	1 Figure measurements	+ 2 Minimum allowances for ease	= 3 Measurements 1 & 2	4 Pattern measurements	5 Alterations
1. Neck A a. At base of neck		0	*		
2. Back Width B–B' a. ½ distance between shoulder tip and underarm seam between marks for armscye. (Approximate 4″ below neck bone.)		¼″ for active garment			

The allowance for ease in column 2 is planned for a suit or coat and will need more ease at some positions.	1 Figure measurements	+ 2 Minimum allowances for ease	= 3 Measurements 1 & 2	4 Pattern measurements	5 Alterations
3. Between ends of shoulder seams. *C–C'*		0			
4. Bust D–D'–D a. Over fullest part.		4″ to 7″			
b. Front bust width to underarm seam. *D–D'*		2″ to 3½″			
c. Back bust width to underarm seams. *D'–D*		2″ to 3½″			
d. Distance down from shoulder to tip of bust along princess line. *E–F*		0			
e. Distance from shoulder over bust tip to waistline. *E–F–G*		Plus ease			
f. High chest measurement close up under arms and above full bust. *H–H'–H*		0			
5. Waistline I–I'–I a. Normal waist or belt line.		Ease up to 1″			
b. Front waistline between underarm seams. *I–I'*		Ease up to ½″			
6. Hips a. 3″ down from waist. *J–J'–J*		1 to 2″			
b. 6″ down from waist. *K–K'–K*		2 to 4″			
c. Around widest hip. *L–L'–L*		3 to 4″			
d. Across front of widest hip. *L–L'*		Depends on flare			
e. Distance down from waistline to widest hip. *G–M*		0			
7. Dress length along center back a. From neckband to waistline. *N–O*		Plus ease			
b. From waistline to finished length along center back. *O–P*		Plus 4″ for hem			
c. Skirt length from floor. *P–Q*					

	1	+	2	=	3	4	5
	Figure measurements		Minimum allowances for ease		Measurements 1 & 2	Pattern measurements	Alterations

The allowance for ease in column 2 is planned for a suit or coat and will need more ease at some positions.

8. Sleeve

a. Place point *R* 2″ below armpit. Place chain around arm parallel to floor and touching *R* and mark *S* on outer arm. *C* to *S* equals height of cap. (Normal measurement range, 5½″ to 6½″. Allow extra the thickness of pad and for cap curve.)	Plus ½″ for arm ease Plus shoulder pad height if used		
b. Outer arm Shoulder tip to bent elbow. *C-T*	½″		
c. Shoulder tip over bent elbow to wrist. *C-T-U*	½″		
d. Around fullest part of upper arm 2″ below armpit. *S-R-S*	3″ or more		
e. Around bent elbow, place tape inside elbow, bend elbow shut, and measure. *T-T′-T*	0		
f. Around wrist, easy measure. *U-U′-U*	To slip hand through easily		

* The first half of space is for *full measurement,* the second half for *half measurement* to use when measuring the pattern.

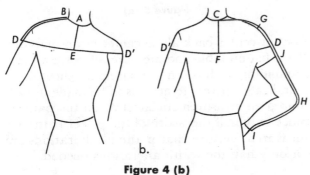

Figure 4 (b)

MEASUREMENT SHEET FOR RAGLAN SLEEVE

Figure 4 b.

	1	+	2	=	3	4	5
	Figure measurements		Minimum allowances for ease		Measurements 1 & 2	Pattern measurements	Alterations

Hold chain around neck and mark
  a. center front
  b. side neck
  c. back neck
Hold chain around width of shoulders, across chest and back. *D-D′-D*			

Measure from neckline to tape along 1. Center front line from neck. *A-E*			
2. Center back line from neck. *C-F*			
3. Shoulder line from neck. *B-D*			
Raise arms out slightly and allow chain to slip through fingers for amount of ease needed around *D-E-D′-F-D*			

Sleeve length

*1. Measure from center back of neck *C*, at bone to shoulder tip *G*, and over bent elbow *H*, to wrist *I*.			
*2. Fullest part of arm (opposite 2 inches below armpit). *J*			
*3. Bent elbow, *H*. (Place tape around elbow, bend forearm up allowing tape to slip through the fingers. This measurement will be minimum girth at elbow.)			
*4. Wrist, *I*. (Plus ease of tape to slip easily over hand.)			

* Same measurement is used for kimono sleeve. If a three-quarter sleeve is used, pin the tape around the arm, the sleeve length desired, and measure from center neck at back along the same positions used for a full-length sleeve, to the desired length.

Measuring the Commercial Pattern

Since commercial patterns vary in size, each pattern used should be carefully measured and checked against figure measurements to insure correct size and fit. This should be done before any alterations are attempted.

All body measurements are taken in full circumference.

Commercial patterns produce only half the figure pattern for the front and back jacket and for skirt; hence care must be taken when reducing the matching figure measurements.

All seam lines should be carefully marked on the pattern so as not to include seams, when measuring the pattern, or all seams may be trimmed away from the pattern edge for measurements.

Surplus tissue around the cutting edges of any pattern pieces should be cut away before trying to use the pattern.

Each grain marking should be ruled the full length of pattern piece for accuracy in measuring.

Use the center front pattern marking for straight grain instead of the grain marking on the pattern front.

Pin in all darts or measure between darts. Pin in all tucks, gathers, pleats and measure across these. All measurements must be taken between seams and recorded in Column 4 on measurement sheet or upon the pattern where alteration is to be made.

Figure 5 a.

Jacket:

Pin the jacket pieces together along all length seams with stitching lines matching. Fold center

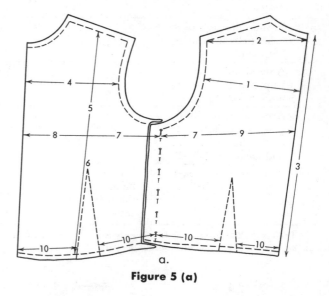

Figure 5 (a)

front or center back along center grain marking. Place flat on table and measure all positions corresponding to those on measurement sheet.

Indicate where alteration is to be made in Column 5 on measurement sheet or on the pattern. Since only half the width of the jacket pattern is measured, be sure that planned alterations are for only half the width alterations needed.

Blouse:

1. Back width between seams.
2. Shoulder tip to shoulder tip.
3. Back length.
4. Chest width.
5. Middle of shoulder to bust tip.
6. From shoulder over bust tip to waistline.
7. Full bust width of front and back.

8. Bust width of front.
9. Bust width of back.
10. Waistline between seams and darts.

Figure 5 b.

Sleeve:

Since grain markings may be slightly off grain in some patterns all sleeve grains should be carefully checked.

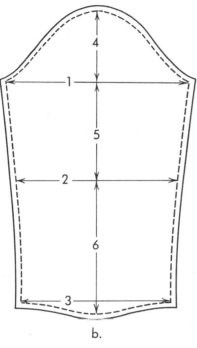

b.

Figure 5 (b)

Fold the one-piece sleeve through length center, matching the stitching lines along length seam and crease. Rule this creased line.

Rule across the base of the sleeve cap from matching stitching points at underarm.

Rule across sleeve at elbow and at wrist.

Place the marked sleeve flat on the table and measure

1. Base of cap between seams.
2. Elbow width between seams.
3. Wrist width between seams.
4. Cap height with ½ inch added for cap curve, and ½ inch to ¾ inch for shoulder pad, if pads are used.
5. Base of cap to elbow.
6. Elbow to wrist. For the full sleeve length, add measurements of 4, 5, and 6.

Figure 5 c.

Two-piece sleeve:

Mark the length grains indicated on upper and under sections of sleeve patterns the full sleeve length.

1. Pin the two back edges of sleeve together almost to elbow with stitching edges matched.
2. Pin two front edges of sleeve together almost to elbow with stitching edges matched.

To secure the base of cap on the upper sleeve section, fold the sleeve so that the underarm grain falls along the upper sleeve grain and mark point X on upper sleeve on length grain, where undersleeve armpit touches grain. This will indicate cap base on upper section.

3. Unpin front seam; place sleeve flat on table for measurement.
   1. Draw cap base line on upper and under sleeve sections at right angles to length grains and measure base of cap between seams.
   2. Elbow width between seams.
   3. Wrist width between seams.
   4. Cap height between seams, plus ½ inch for cap curve and ½ inch to ¾ inch for shoulder pad if pads are used.
   5. Cap to elbow.
   6. Elbow to wrist between seams.

Add measurements 4, 5, and 6 for the full sleeve length.

Figure 5 d.

Skirt:

Pin front skirt sections together with stitching edges matching.

Pin back skirt sections together with stitching edges matching.

Pin front and back skirt sections together along side seams to just below the widest hip having stitching edges matching. This allows skirt to lie flat on the table without curling up from table.

Measure:

1. Waist of front and back between seams and darts.
   Front waist.
   Back waist.

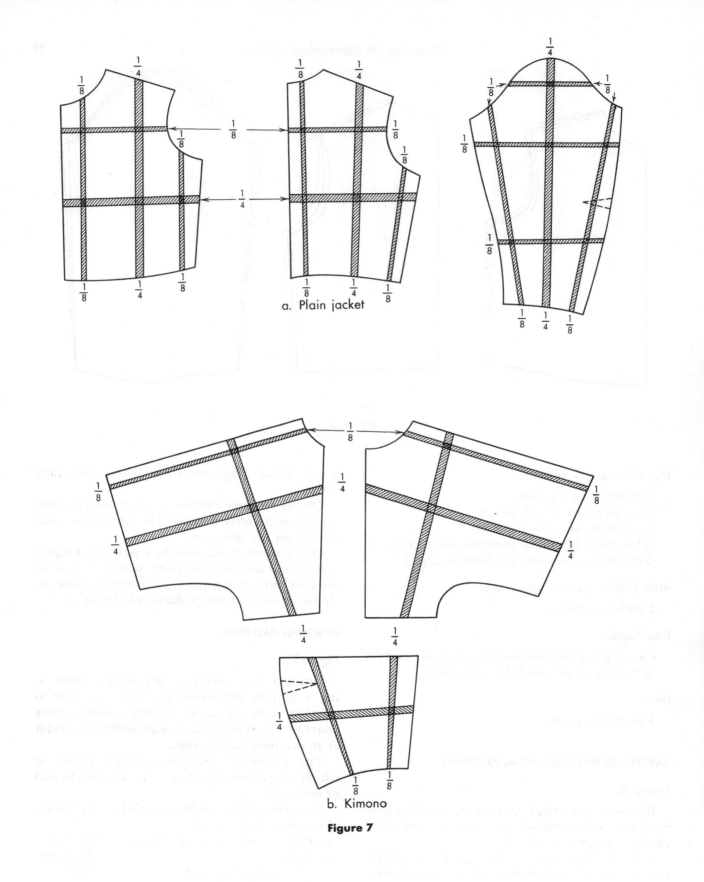

a. Plain jacket

b. Kimono

Figure 7

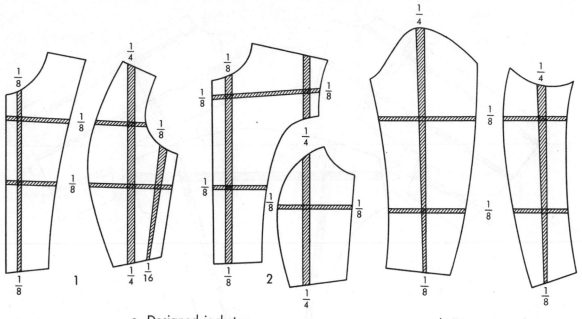

c. Designed jackets   d. Two-piece sleeve

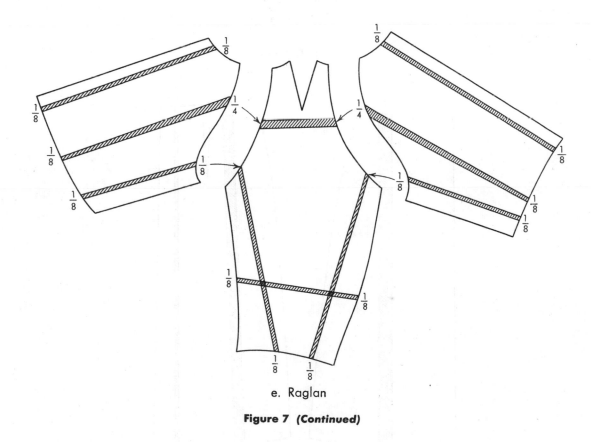

e. Raglan

Figure 7 (Continued)

23

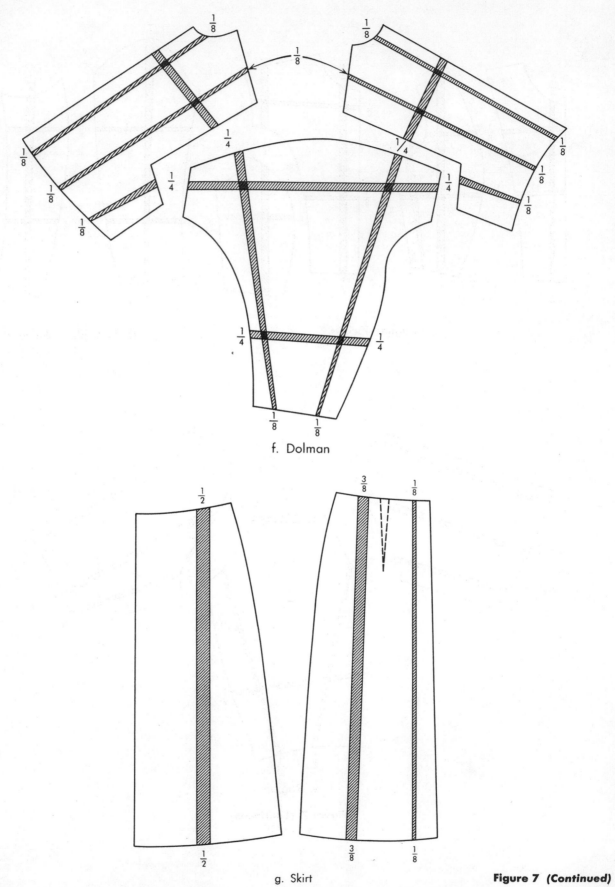

f. Dolman

g. Skirt

Figure 7 (Continued)

Pattern Alteration

Because commercial patterns are made for the ideal figure, almost all patterns will need some alteration owing to figure variances.

Most of the problems in fitting can be eliminated by taking careful measurements of both figure and pattern.

By comparing figure and pattern measurements, one can decide the amount of increase or decrease of the pattern size.

Additional seam allowances may be chalked on the fabric after the pattern is pinned to the fabric, but all other pattern alterations should be made on the pattern before it is pinned to the fabric.

DARTS (FOUR MAIN POSITIONS)

Figure 8.

Darts are used in garment construction to allow ease over curved portions of the figure. A single dart or a combination of darts may be used, depending upon the amount of ease needed.

Concealed darts may appear in the structural lines of a garment as in Figure 9.

For a very full-busted figure it is advisable to use a shoulder dart plus an additional dart elsewhere on the garment in order to keep the grain of the garment hanging correctly.

    a. All stitched darts in the jacket front point toward the bust tip, but end before reaching the bust tip as indicated in the dotted lines in figure.

        Instead of stitched darts, tucks or gathers may be used at the shoulder, or at the waistline.

The following four main darts, or a combination of two of them, are most commonly used in patterns.

    b. Shows the position for slashing to transfer a dart position.

        1. Waistline dart position.

        2. Diagonal underarm dart position.

        3. Underarm dart.

        4. Shoulder dart.

These darts may be used singly, or in combinations on one garment as follows:

    1 and 3—waistline and underarm darts.

    1 and 4—waistline and shoulder darts.

    2 and 4—diagonal underarm and shoulder darts.

    3 and 4—underarm and shoulder darts.

For the very full-busted figure, a shoulder dart is essential to keep the grain of jacket straight. A second dart may be used at any other position desired. Since the underarm dart is the shortest of all darts, it is usually broken down into two or three darts. Not more than ¾ inch should be taken into one dart, making the stitched dart ⅜ inch on wrong side.

    c. Shows the waistline dart pinned out.

    d. Shows the spread of the new dart position.

    e. Shows the diagonal underarm dart pinned out and transferred to the underarm dart position.

    f. Shows the underarm dart pinned out and transferred to the shoulder dart position.

Any dart in a jacket front may be pinned out and transferred to any position without following the sequence given above.

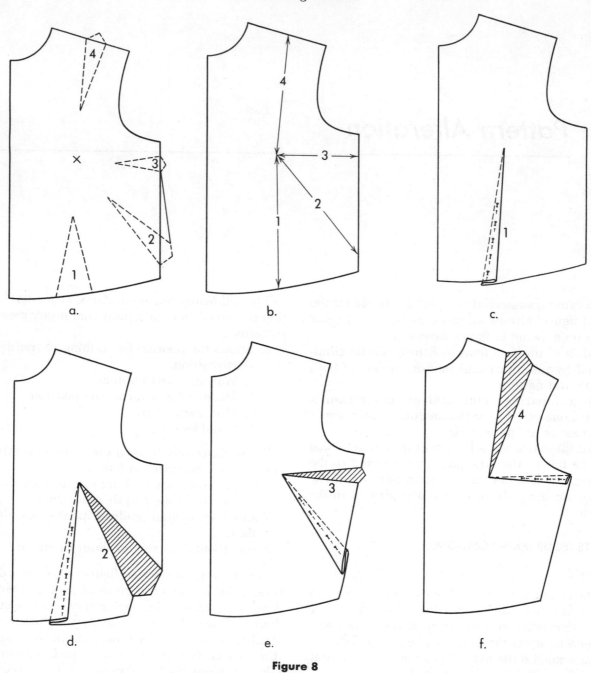

Figure 8

OTHER DART POSITIONS USED IN GARMENT CONSTRUCTION

Figure 9.

Design lines of a garment frequently conceal the position of a dart, incorporating it in the design line. Darts may also be used at other positions on a figure as shown in a few diagrams in the following figures:

a. In a coat or suit, a dart is frequently concealed under the collar, dropping down from the neck edge. Frequently a second dart may appear elsewhere on the garment or be worked out in the construction lines of the garment.

b. When a yoke is used, the dart may be incorporated in the construction line from the armscye line.

a.   b.   c.

d.   e.

Figure 9

c. In a princess line the dart is fitted out in the construction line, part at the shoulder and part at the waistline.
d. When a garment has the design line curving from the armscye down into the waistline, part of the dart is fitted out at armscye and part at waistline position.
e. If the garment has a design of crossbands, part of the dart is fitted out at the armscye edge, and part at the underarm dart.

Figure 9 f.

Flange or shoulder edge dart:

This dart is used in dressmaker suits and is good for a full-busted person where a shoulder dart is needed and where one wants softness instead of a tailored effect.

1. Slash front ¼ inch in and parallel to armscye 6 inches down, then diagonally to bust tip.

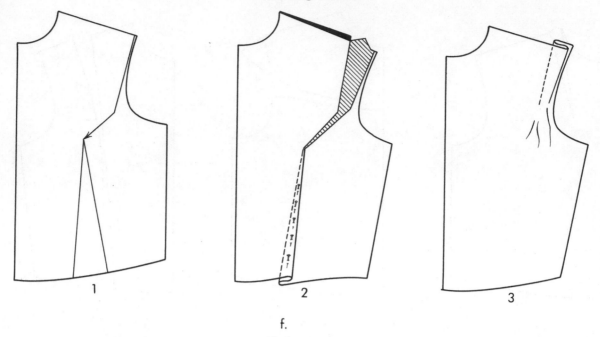

f.

Figure 9 (f)

Fold in waist dart or any other dart position, and allow shoulder dart to spread until pattern lies flat.
2. Fill in new shoulder dart with pattern tissue.
3. Fold dart edges together and stitch down 5 inches, leaving dart free below.

These are only a few designs showing positions where darts may be used in the construction lines of a garment.

Figure 10.

Dart at back of neck:

a. Mark the center back halfway between neck edge and waistline.

Place center back along the ruled edge of pattern tissue and draw around pattern. Hold the marked center of back length to the tissue and swing the upper half of pattern outward ½ inch to widen neck edge of back. Draw new upper back along pattern edge.

b. Measure 1 inch in on neck line from new center back and mark. Draw line 2½ or 3 inches down from this mark and parallel to center back for dart position. Fold along dart line and make dart ¼ inch at top running off to nothing at bottom. This dart may be made into two small darts if desired.

Dart at shoulder line:

c. All one-piece-back jackets have ease at the waistline which may be gathered or made into one or two darts above the waist. Fold into ½ inch of dart at waist. From top end of dart draw a line up through the center of shoulder seam.

d. Cut from shoulder to dart end along drawn line and spread ½ to ¾ inch at shoulder seam. The pattern should lie flat on the table. Fill in the shoulder-dart spread with pattern tissue.

e. Mark dart length 2½ or 3 inches down from shoulder, using dart width at shoulder, running off to nothing at end.

ENLARGED BUST ALTERATION

Figure 11.

a. Rule and cut through front pattern along bust line from center front to within ¼ inch of the underarm pattern edge, and from the middle of shoulder seam through tip of bust to within ¼ inch of waistline edge of pattern.

b. Pin lower center front pattern along a ruled edge of pattern tissue. Swing armscye and underarm section away from lower front section allowing ½ of the bust increase needed at the intersection of the two cut

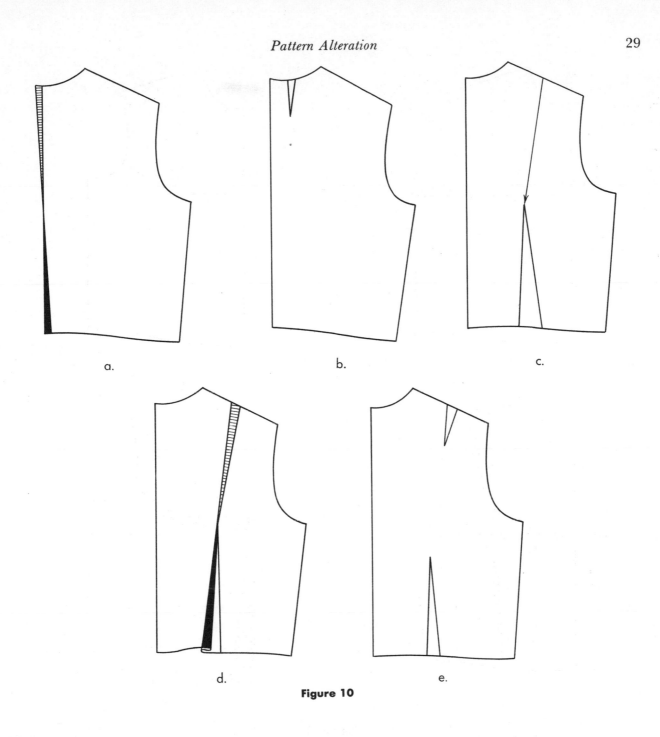

a.

b.

c.

d.

e.

Figure 10

lines at bust tip. Pin this lower side section and armscye section to paper with the inner edge of each along a ruled line. Place the upper front neck section with the center front along the ruled edge of pattern tissue, allowing spread from tip of bust to center front and keeping the shoulder line straight from neck edge to shoulder tip.

This increases the width and length over the bust, also adds a new dart at the shoulder seam. This alteration is used for a full-busted person.

If only a slight increase is needed in the bust, the following alteration may be used. This alteration swings the increased dart at the waistline, but this dart may be transferred elsewhere on the pattern if desired.

  c. Slash the jacket front from center front straight out to the tip of bust, then diagonally to within ¼ inch of armscye.

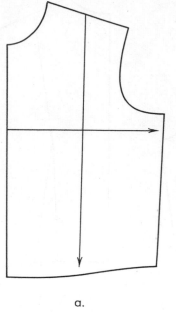

a.

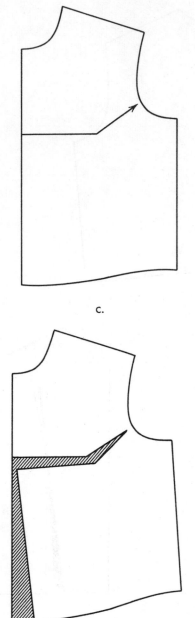

c.

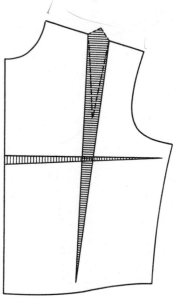

b.

d.

Figure 11

d. Pin upper front section along ruled line on new tissue. Swing the lower front section away from the center front ruled line until ½ of the desired increase appears at the upper center front spread, and pin the lower section into place. The increase at lower center front waistline may be incorporated in a dart at the normal waistline dart position, or may be transferred to any other dart.

ROUND SHOULDER ALTERATION

Figure 12.

A round-shouldered figure increases in width across the upper shoulders, also in back length from shoulders to waistline.

a. Rule and cut along back bust line of blouse, or 2 inches below underarm, from center back to within ¼ inch of the underarm seam.

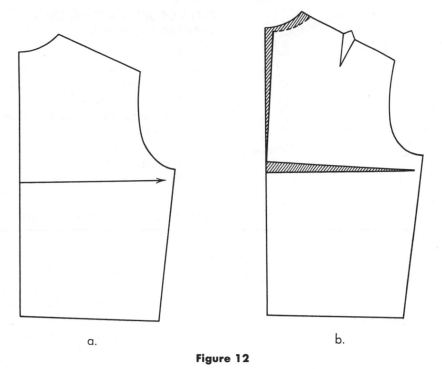

a.   b.

Figure 12

b. Pin lower back section to a ruled line of pattern tissue. Raise upper back section, swinging center back away from the new pattern edge to widen the upper back one half of the desired back increase.

Draw around entire new pattern edge as shown by broken edge line.

This alteration has increased the back neck width which must be reduced to the original size.

Remove the original upper back section, place it on the new pattern with shoulder edges touching new shoulder line and center back falling on center back ruled line. Redraw a new neck line to replace that increased during alteration.

The shoulder seam has been increased in length.

Place a dart halfway between neck edge and shoulder tip to use up this increase. This dart is 2½ or 3 inches long and the point of dart should swing ¼ inch toward the center back, off the straight grain of material.

If the fabric shrinks easily, the excess shoulder length may be eased onto the front shoulder.

WIDEN SHOULDERS

Figure 13.

a. Rule back jacket pattern and cut 1 inch within shoulder line on back parallel to center back to 1 inch below bust line, then straight out, almost to underarm seam.

b. Place back pattern on new paper and spread cut section to desired shoulder width and pin into position.

Rule from neck edge to shoulder tip for new shoulder line. The front of the pattern must also be made wider to care for the shoulder width, so the same width alteration must be made on the front pattern to match the back alteration. Repeat exactly the same alteration on the front jacket, in the same position from armscye.

NARROW SHOULDERS

Figure 14.

a. Rule and cut 1 inch within shoulder line on back parallel to center back to 1 inch below bust line, then straight out almost to underarm seams.

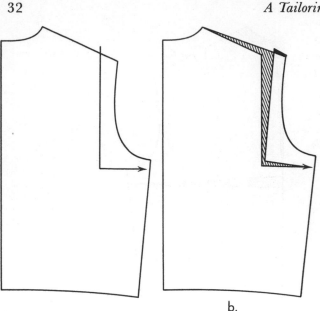

Figure 13

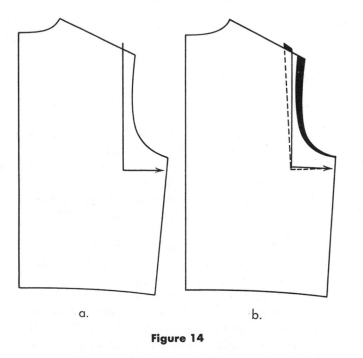

Figure 14

TYPES OF SET-IN SLEEVES USED IN TAILORED GARMENTS

Figure 15.

a. Plain sleeve with darts from wrist to elbow.

b. Bell sleeve.

c. Sleeve with dart or darts at elbow.

d. Two-piece sleeve, most commonly used in a jacket.

e. Sleeve with seam down center, commonly used in a coat.

f. Sleeve with darts at shoulder, used occasionally when fashion dictates.

SLEEVE CAP INCREASE IN HEIGHT

Figure 16 a, b.

a. AB Length grain of sleeve.

To secure, fold sleeve lengthwise with stitching corners matching at armpit and length seams falling flush.

CD Cap base. Draw line at cap base connecting the two underarm stitching corners at armpit.

E Intersection of AB and CD.

AE Cap height.

F 1½ inches from A on sleeve cap.

G 1½ inches from A on sleeve cap.

H 2 inches below C.

I 2 inches below D.

Connect FI.

Connect GH.

J Intersection of FI and GH.

Slash along line from F to within ⅛ inch of I.

Slash along line from G to within ⅛ inch of H.

b. Raise wedge $FAGJ$ above point J the desired amount of cap height increase, keeping line AJ on the center sleeve line AB.

K ½ of CF.

L ½ of GD.

Slash sleeve section up to within ⅛ inch of K.

Slash sleeve section up to within ⅛ inch of L.

Raise the two side sections of sleeve cap until the cap top curves smoothly into the wedge.

This new cap formed should give desired height and add some width, which is always needed with an increased cap height.

b. Place pattern on new paper and overlap cut section on back to desired back width and pin into position. Rule from neck edge to shoulder tip for new shoulder line.

Repeat exactly the same alteration on the front jacket. Rule new shoulder line from neck edge to shoulder tip. Fill in or cut away surplus seam.

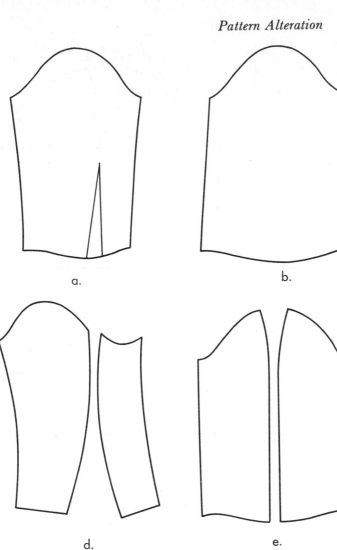

a.   b.   c.

d.   e.   f.

Figure 15

SLEEVE CAP INCREASE OF SLEEVE WITH SEAM AT CENTER

Figure 16 c, d.

c. AB Length grain.
The two sleeve sections are placed ¼ inch apart with sleeve grain parallel to AB.

CD Cap base. Connect the two stitching corners at armpit.

E Intersection of AB and CD.

F Top of back half of sleeve cap.

G Top of front half of sleeve.

H 1½ inches from G.

I 1½ inches from F.

J 2 inches down from C.

K 2 inches down from D.
Connect HK.
Connect IJ.

L Intersection of HK and IJ.
Slash along line from H to within ⅛ inch of K.
Slash along line from I to within ⅛ inch of J.

d.   On sleeve sections raise wedges GHL and FIL the desired cap height increase, keeping the sides GL and FL the same distance from line AB.

M ½ of CH.

N ½ of ID.
Slash sleeve section up to within ⅛ inch of M.
Slash sleeve section up to within ⅛ inch of N.
Raise the two side sections of the sleeve cap until the cap edge curves smoothly into the two raised wedges.
Connect sections by dotted line to

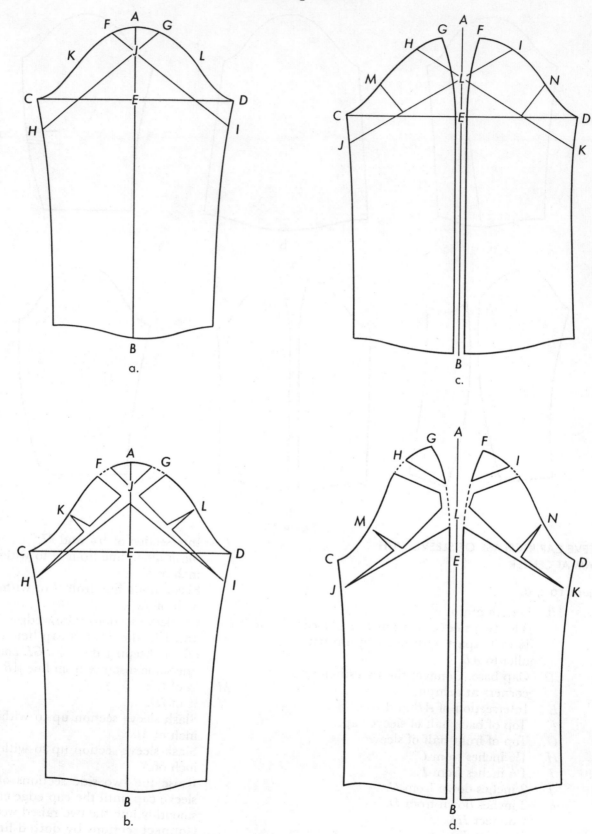

Figure 16

wedges. This new cap formed should give the desired cap height and add some width, which is needed with an increased cap height.

SLEEVE CAP INCREASE FOR A TWO-PIECE SLEEVE

Figure 16 e, f.

e.   *AB*   Length grain of the upper sleeve section.

     C   End of stitching seam on back edge of upper sleeve section.

     D   End of stitching seam on front edge of upper arm section.

     EF   Length grain of under sleeve section.

     G   End of stitching seam on front edge of under sleeve section.

     H   Edge of armscye touching line *EF* at underarm.

     I   Edge of armscye touching line *EF* at underarm.

     J   End of stitching seam on back edge of undersleeve section.

f.   Cut under sleeve section along *EF,* making it into two sections.

Match point *J* to *C,* allowing sleeve stitching lines to touch downward toward the elbow.

Match point *G* to *D,* allowing sleeve stitching lines to touch downward toward the elbow.

Connect points *H* and *I.* This line formed is the cap base and should be at right angles to line *AB.*

     K   Intersection of *AB* and *IH.*

Figure 16 g.

g.   *AB*   Length grain of sleeve.

     IH   Cap base.

     K   Intersection of *AB* and *IH.*

     AK   Cap height.

     L   1½ inches from *A* on sleeve cap.

     M   1½ inches from *A* on sleeve cap.

     N   2 inches below *I.*

     O   2 inches below *H.*

Connect *MN.*

Connect *LO.*

     P   Intersection of *MN* and *LO.*

Slash along line from *M* to within ⅛ inch of *N.*

Slash along line from *L* to within ⅛ inch of *O.*

Raise wedge *LAMP* just above point *P* the desired amount of cap height increase, keeping line *AP* on the center sleeve line *AB.*

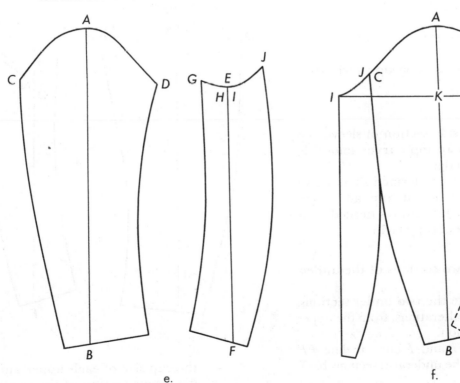

e.   f.

Figure 16 (Continued)

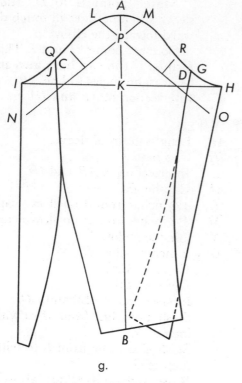

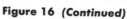

g.

Figure 16 (Continued)

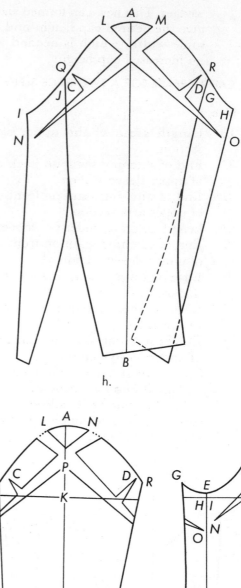

h.

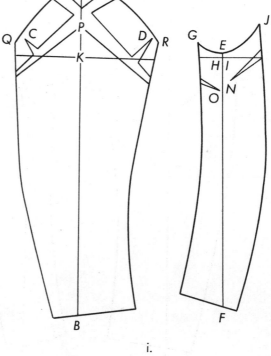

i.

Q   ½ of *IL*.
R   ½ of *MH*.
     Slash sleeve section up to within ⅛ inch of *Q*.
     Slash sleeve section up to within ⅛ inch of *R*.

Figure 16 h.

h.   Raise the side section of sleeve cap until the cap top curves smoothly into the wedge.

      This new cap formed should give the desired height and add some width, which is always needed with an increase of cap height.

Figure 16 i.

i.   Join the two sections of the under-sleeve.

      Separate the two under sections, with their alterations, from the upper sleeve section.

      Match *H* and *I* back to line *EF* and paste the underarm sections back together.

      This increase formed has increased the cap size of each upper and under sleeve section of the two-piece sleeve.

Making the Muslin Garment

To eliminate any hazards in construction, it is wise to construct a muslin jacket or upper part of a coat before cutting into the fabric itself. In a coat of princess lines, the entire garment should be made first in muslin. Although this method takes somewhat longer in the construction process, it is justified because it eliminates the possibility of mistakes likely to occur with even the most careful sewer.

Heavy unbleached muslin or similar material is used for this purpose. The muslin is cut from the altered pattern, marked, and basted (using long machine stitch or hand basting). The muslin garment is fitted as accurately as the garment itself. The collar and both sleeves are fitted into the garment.

The muslin should be torn across each end, pulled into shape, and pressed before any cutting is done. It should be folded right side in, so that all markings, except center front and back, appear on wrong side.

Spread the muslin on the cutting table with selvage parallel to table edge and torn ends parallel to the end of the table.

Plan the entire pattern layout on the muslin before pinning into place and check carefully the grain of the pattern with that of the muslin. Pin each pattern piece to the muslin before cutting.

Carefully mark the entire cut garment before removing the pattern.

On the muslin, the stitching lines may be marked along a ruled line with a tracing wheel or pencil.

For additional seam allowances, mark along ruled line, except for curved edges.

Refer to page 38 for suggested seam allowances, and mark seams out beyond muslin edge before cutting. Cut the entire muslin garment.

All edge notches should be cut *out of* instead of *into* the seam edge.

All length grains are marked along a ruled line on the muslin since the muslin will be used in place of the tissue when cutting the wool garment.

CUTTING THE MUSLIN JACKET

For cutting one should use shears about 8 inches long, with sharp edges and a fine point for clipping. Cutting should be done with fabric lying flat on the table and with the full length of the blade.

If a muslin jacket or coat is made prior to the wool garment, no cutting is planned on the wool before the muslin has been cut, fitted, and adjusted. This muslin is then used as a part of the pattern in the garment layout.

It is not advisable to use pinking shears when cutting out a garment for one does not get as clean-cut an edge as with shears. Also, all garment edges will not need to be pinked, especially those covered with a lining.

The pinked edge should be made after the seam is stitched so that the edge will be parallel to the stitched seam.

SUGGESTED ALLOWANCES FOR FINISHED SEAMS AND HEMS

Inches	
1 to 1½	Fitting seams
	Shoulder
	Underarm
	Sleeve
¾ to 1	Design seams
½	Neck
½	Armscye
½	Waistline
	Hem finishes
1½ or more	Jacket and coat sleeves
2 to 3	Wide coat or jacket sleeve
1½ or more	Jacket hem
2 to 3	Coat hem. Allow 1 extra inch for hanging
2 to 3	Skirt hem. Allow 1 extra inch for hanging

MARKING THE GARMENT

Figure 17.

Tailor tacks are made through two thicknesses of material on tucks, darts, pleats, buttonholes, and buttons. Sometimes tailor tacks are made along the stitching edges of wool garments so that the two portions of the garment are marked identically.

If tailor tacks are made of contrasting darning cotton, take only one stitch as it does not slide from the fabric. If made of a basting thread, take two tiny stitches through the two thicknesses, leaving a loop and thread ends about ½ inch long on the wrong side of the garment.

The two sections of the garment are then separated and the tacks cut between, leaving matching thread tacks on each section. These tacks are left permanently in muslin for reference, and in the wool garment until ready for permanent stitching.

Long and short bastings are used down the center front and back of each garment piece. These bastings are left in until the garment is finished.

Figure 18.

The sleeve is marked with long and short basting:

a. The entire center grain length.
b. Base of the cap from stitching points or armcap to armcap on underarm seams.
c. A basting 2 inches above and parallel to *b.*
d. A basting 2 inches above and parallel to *c.*

These sleeve bastings are used to keep the grain straight when fitting sleeve into armscye.

BASTING THE JACKET

For fitting, all bastings should be done with short even stitches, using heavy-duty thread that is stronger and smoother than regular white basting cotton. A contrasting color is advisable, for it is more easily seen than a matching color. On white or pastels, a pastel-colored thread should be used as some dark colors may crock and stain the fabric when steamed.

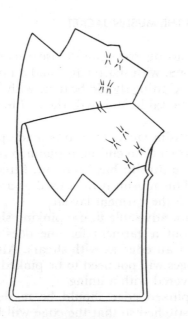

Figure 17

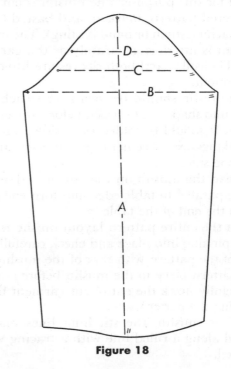

Figure 18

In a garment with set-in sleeves, the sleeves are not basted into the garment for the first fitting.

In the raglan, kimono, or dolman, the sleeves are basted into position for the first fitting.

For the first and all subsequent fittings, shoulder pads of the correct size and shape *must* be used.

Baste all darts or tucks in front, back, and sleeve, using small basting stitches.

Carefully match stitching edges together and pin, with pins at right angles to the cut edges, and baste with short bastings along stitching edges.

Baste the following seams:

1. Yokes to garment section.
2. Princess seams, if used.
3. Lengthwise back seams.
4. Underarm seams, leaving darts standing free.
5. Shoulder seams, leaving darts standing free. Ease back shoulder seam onto the front shoulder seam.
6. Lengthwise sleeve edges with darts standing free.

FITTING THE JACKET OR COAT

A suit jacket should be fitted over a blouse or sweater; and a coat should be fitted over a dress or over a suit, if suits are to be worn under the coat.

Adjust the garment to the figure and pin the center fronts together the entire length of the garment.

Insert the shoulder pads from the armscye edge of the garment, allowing the straight thick edge of the pad to extend ½ inch (or as fashion dictates) outside the armscye stitching line. Pin the pads into position.

When fitting a garment, stand behind or at the side of the model, with the model facing a full-length mirror. This position permits both persons to see fitting process in the mirror.

Fit the garment in the following order: the back shoulders, front shoulders, then the underarm seams.

The garment should fit the figure smoothly, without any wrinkles and with center front and center back bastings and side seams hanging perpendicular to the floor. See fitting problems on the following pages.

If one shoulder is lower than the other, the low shoulder should be built up with more wadding in the shoulder pad or one of the pads should be reduced in thickness.

If bust, chest, or other parts of the figure need wadding to smooth out the figure, these sections should be cared for in this first fitting.

See padding problems in Fig. 20, p. 42.

When the garment has been rebasted after the first fitting, it should be tried on and carefully checked to insure a correct fit before any stitching is done.

SELF FITTING

If one has to do her own fitting, she will find as an excellent aid a dress form which is made over her own figure.

Directions for the dress form are given on p. 9. If a dress form is not available, one can use the trial and error method. This, of course, means trying on many times but can be successful if one is patient.

To fit a skirt, first measure the belt around the waist and baste across the two matching ends; also mark second side seam, center front, and back with bastings. Pin the skirt to the belt before trying on for first fitting. Try on and fit skirt down to widest hips. Remove, baste fitted section, then rule remaining seams up from skirt bottom and continue basting with the grain. Try on for readjustments.

To hang the skirt, adjust to the figure, use table edge as a guide, and mark with pins around the skirt at table top. Measure from table edge to floor, subtract the distance from floor that the skirt is to be worn, and measure skirt hem edge parallel to pins at hip.

Adjust the jacket and pin opening. Adjust shoulder pads and pin into place. Fit one shoulder and underarm, remove, and pin second side to match the fitted one. Try on for additional adjustments.

Pin and baste collar into place, then try on to check for accuracy. Remove to make adjustments.

Mark the armscye by placing one pin at shoulder tip, one at chest width, and one at underarm. Remove and try back width the same as chest width marking. Connect the four pin markings with basting, keeping a good armscye shape.

Use a dress form or pad a coat hanger with a turkish towel to simulate a shoulder.

Place garment on one or the other and pin upper half of sleeve into place, remove, and pin under section. Baste into place and try on for fit,

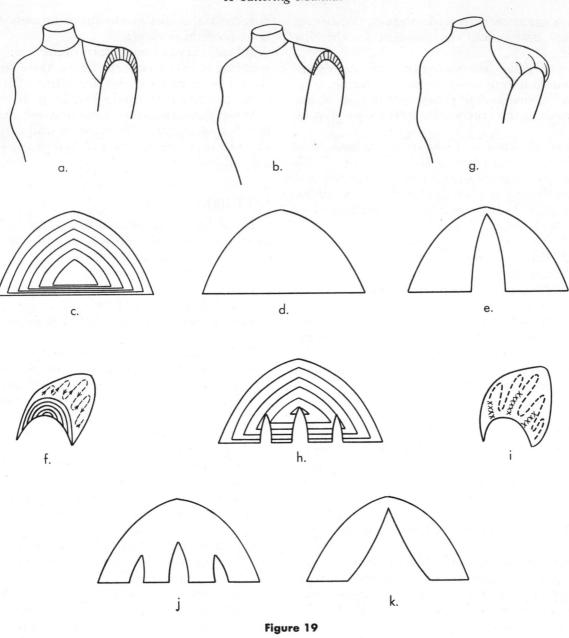

Figure 19

marking with pins any points which need adjustment. Remove and adjust until you reach a correct fit.

SHOULDER PADS

Figure 19.

Shoulder pads are used in tailored garments to give a smooth finish at shoulder and armscye and should be used for each fitting of the garment. The size varies with current fashion, type of garment, and the slope of the wearer's shoulder.

Pads may be purchased ready-made or be made by the individual.

Materials needed are cotton or felt wadding, crinoline, canvas, muslin.

a, b. Normal shoulder pads in two thicknesses.

c. Wadding cut with decreasing sizes until it is the desired thickness.

d. Crinoline for top covering.

e. Canvas for underside with dart to reduce size for inside curve.

f. Wadding curved over the hand while sewing together. Begin at center and stab stitch the wadding sections together, curving larger sections downward overhand as you stitch.

Begin at center and repeat for second side.

Crinoline and canvas cover top and bottom and are sewn by hand or machine around curved edge.

g. Figure shows pad used in a drop shoulder or raglan sleeve.

h. Wadding is cut with greatest thickness at shoulder edge and tapered toward neck and outer edge.

Darts are cut from lower edge and wadding edges are drawn together and sewn, but not overlapped.

i. Stab stitch wadding thickness together, beginning at center, and curve overhand as you continue stitching. Repeat for second side.

j. Crinoline with darts to curve over shoulder.

k. Canvas with large dart to curve for underside of pad.

FIGURE PROBLEMS

Figure 20.

1 Problem: Lower back armscye of pattern is cut too deep and is tight across lower back armscye. (Stout persons with narrow shoulders and wide lower backs frequently have this problem.)

Widen the lower half of armscye from back width to armpit up to ½ inch.

Widen the sleeve section which fits along the widened armscye edge of the jacket up to ½ inch.

If the above alteration is too much, the excess may be fitted out when the sleeve is fitted into the armscye.

Figure peculiarities can be overcome and made to look better proportioned and attractive if some padding is done in the garment. This padding is made of cotton or felted wadding to the correct size and thickness and is sewn into place within the garment.

2 Problem: A flat-busted figure.

Fill out bust in the jacket with bust pads sewn to the canvas between the canvas and the lining. These pads are made by cutting decreasing circles which are stacked together until right thickness is reached, then stab stitched together. Results produce a better proportioned figure.

3 Problem: Very full low bust with hollow between bust and armscye.

Fill in hollow until line from shoulder to bust tip is straight, using wadding of cotton or felt. This will reduce the apparent bust size. Sew the wadding to the canvas between canvas and lining.

4 Problem: Hollow chest.

Fill in the chest hollows where needed with two or three thicknesses of wadding, shape as desired, and sew to canvas.

5 Problem: One shoulder lower than the other.

Add enough extra wadding to shoulder pad to equalize the two shoulders. See shoulder pads in Fig. 19, p. 40.

6 Problem: Hollow below back waist and large *derrière*.

Make covered pad of correct shape, size, and thickness and attach at lower inside edge of belt.

GARMENT PROBLEMS IN FITTING

Figure 21.

1 Problem: Back neck of garment too wide.

a. Neck edge at the back of the garment is too wide and stands away from the body. Some of it may be eased onto the neck finish but the surplus will need to be fitted out.

b. Two darts, one on either side of the center back, might be used. Measure 2½ inches out from the center back at neck and 3 inches down below neck edge and mark. Make two small darts ⅛ inch at top and tapering to nothing 3 inches down from neck.

c. The excess fullness may be fitted out down from the neck if garment has a seam at center back.

d. The upper back may be recut. Rip apart shoulder and underarm seams. Place the back pattern down from the shoulder and neck edge and recut the upper back, decreasing the neck width the desired amount. Rebaste and check for correct fit.

2 Problem: Wrinkles below collar at upper back.

a. Wrinkles across back below neck seam.

b. Neck seam may be too tight and needs clipping to ease.

c. Back shoulder seam too tight on front seam.

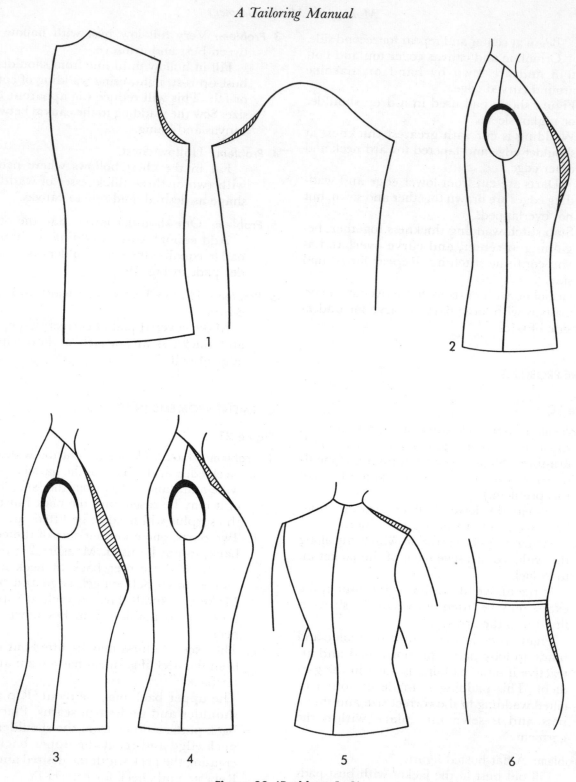

Figure 20 (Problems 1-6)

Rip and ease back seam on to front seam.

d. Shoulder high at shoulder tip. Rip seam and let out more at shoulder from neck toward shoulder tip.

3 Problem: Round shoulder.

a. Garment bunches at armscye below back width.

b. Rip shoulder seam, raise armscye edge until

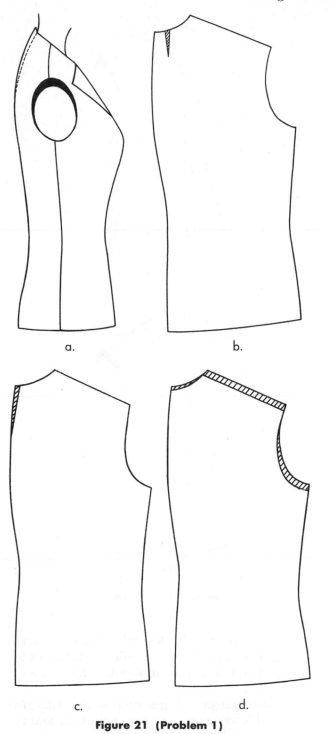

a.

b.

c.

d.

Figure 21 (Problem 1)

4 *Problem:* Full bust.

    a. Garment bunches may appear at front armscye as in 3, Round shoulders, *a* above.

    b. Rip shoulder seam, raise jacket until smooth along armscye, swing slightly in toward neck at shoulder, and add excess shoulder length into shoulder dart.

       If there is no shoulder dart, the excess may be made into a small dart under the collar.

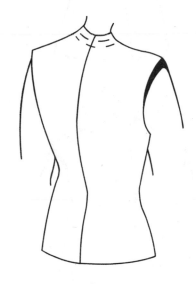

a.

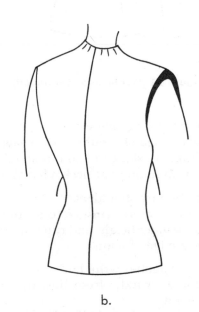

b.

Figure 21 (Problem 2)

smooth along armscye, swing armscye edge over slightly toward neck along shoulder seam, and make dart at shoulder center. This raises back seam higher at shoulder tip than front shoulder seam and disposes of extra armscye length.

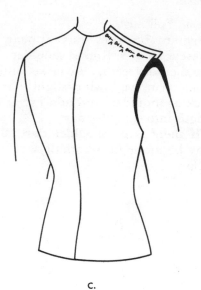

c.

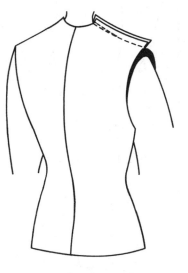

d.

Figure 21 (Problem 2, Continued)

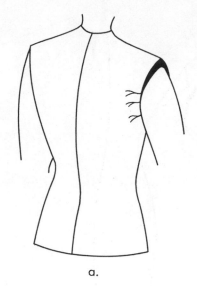

a.

b.

Figure 21 (Problem 3)

5 Problem: Sloping shoulders.

Armscye edge of shoulder seam sags on figure. Take up slack in seam at shoulder and
run out to nothing at neck edge of seam.

6 Problem: Square shoulders.

Let out seam at armscye to accommodate
extra shoulder height and run out to nothing
at neck edge of seam.

7 Problem: Diagonal wrinkles.

a. Diagonal wrinkles from bust tip to underarm seam.

b. Pin tuck across one half of back width until
diagonal wrinkles disappear from front.

Pin same size tuck in original back pattern.

Rip shoulder seam, fold back halves together, and pin along shoulder and armscye
edges.

c. Place pattern on garment with underarm
and lower armscye edges matching and recut shoulder and neck.

Rebaste and fit garment.

d. Rip underarm seam to width of bust line.
Raise front underarm seam until diagonal
wrinkles disappear and make small underarm dart.

Refit underarm seam below dart. This
fitting narrows the front pattern below the

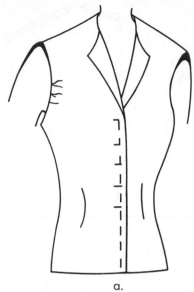

a.

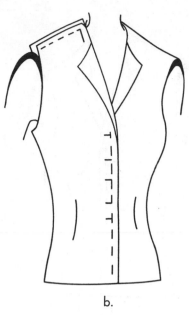

b.

Figure 21 (Problem 4)

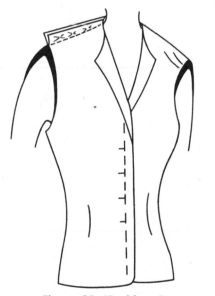

Figure 21 (Problem 5)

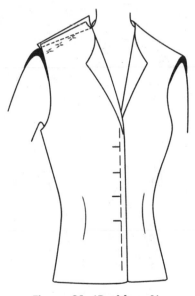

Figure 21 (Problem 6)

bust line but should not be used if it distorts the design of the garment.

8 Problem: Back of princess or fitted garment too long from neck to waist and wrinkles across shoulders.

Use the same alteration as 7 *a, b,* and *c* to remove excess back length.

9 Problem: Garment too wide both front and back.

  a. Pin out surplus front and back in a tuck from shoulder down to bottom of jacket.

Transfer same size tuck to pattern front and back.

Release tuck in garment. Rip side seams. Fold garment down center front and back.

  b. Pin pattern to garment with center fronts and center backs matching and recut along armscye and side seams.

Rebaste garment for second fitting.

10 Problem: Entire bust too tight.

Rip underarm seam and let out both front and back seams.

a.

b.

Figure 21 (Problem 7)

c.

d.

Figure 21 (Problem 7d)

Figure 21 (Problem 8)

11 Problem: Entire bust too large but shoulder width correct.

Take up underarm seams. This reduces the armscye, which may be increased by clipping around the underarm curve to give the desired ease.

12 Problem: Underarm dart too low or too high.

With garment on the figure, mark with a row of pins the new bust line dart opposite the tip of bust and parallel to the floor.

Remove garment; rip underarm darts

and seam along darts and raise or lower the dart to the new marked position.

13 Problem: Hollow chest, with wrinkles appearing below the shoulder seam.

Rip shoulder seam to within ½ inch of the neck edge.

Smooth front shoulder section out toward shoulder tip and repin shoulder seam. Mark new stitching line of front upper armscye with pins, and trim away any excess material.

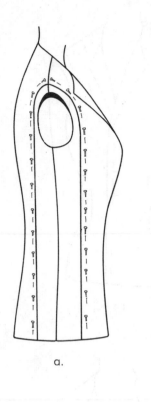

a.

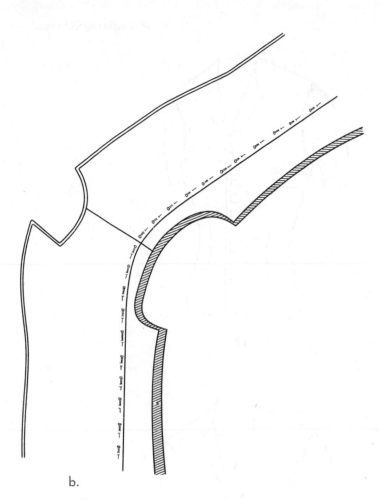

b.

Figure 21 (Problem 9)

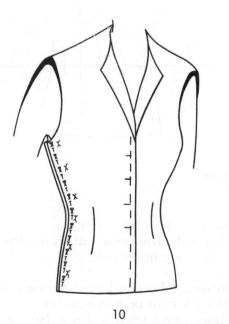

10

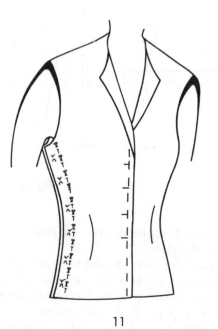

11

Figure 21 (Problems 10, 11)

47

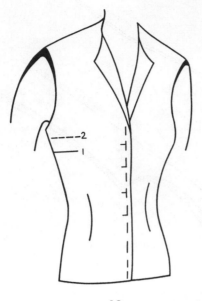

12

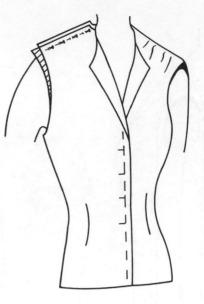

13

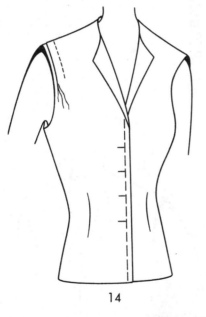

14

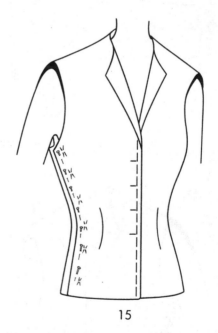

15

Figure 21 (Problems 12, 13, 14, 15)

14 Problem: Shoulders too narrow on a full-busted figure.

A shoulder dart should be used, preferably a flange dart at armscye edge which gives the appearance of widening the shoulders. See Fig. 9, p. 28, for directions.

Lines in the design of the garment should be selected to give the appearance of widened shoulders.

15 Problem: Front bust too tight.

Rip underarm seam and let out front seam only along underarm.

16 Problem: Kimono-sleeved garment too long in back from neck to waistline.

a. Take a tuck from width of back at center back upward to shoulder line about 2 inches beyond the shoulder tip, decreasing the tuck

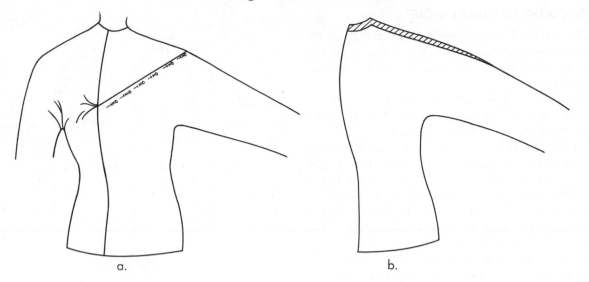

Figure 21 (Problem 16)

in width toward shoulder edge. The shoulder line from neck to elbow may need to be straightened out after the tuck is formed if the continuous line is disturbed.

Pin a tuck at the same position and of same size in the back tissue pattern. Remove the tuck from the garment, rip the shoulder seams, and fold the back down center back with all shoulder edges matching.

b. Fit the lower back and sleeve of pattern to garment and cut away surplus at neck and shoulder.

17 Problem: Armscye of garment too tight and tends to fold over at underarm, or is too high and binds the underarm.

a. Clip ¼ inch in around lower underarm section of one armscye and, if necessary, continue clipping ⅛ inch more until armscye is of correct size.

b. Turn down clipped sections and pin each section to garment to check. When the arm is held down, the underarm of garment should stand straight up without breaking.

Mark final stitching line with row of pins a seam's width from fold. The armpit to underarm stitching line should measure 2 to 3 inches for a normal suit sleeve, more for a coat.

Remove garment and baste around the *one marked sleeve.* Fold garment, matching shoulder and underarm seams and armhole edges, and transfer same markings to the second armscye.

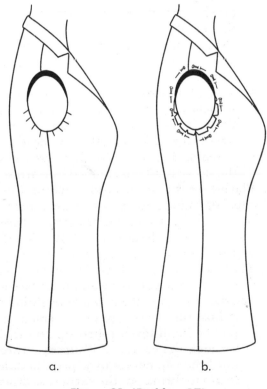

Figure 21 (Problem 17)

BASTE COLLAR TO MUSLIN JACKET

The neck of the garment is larger than the collar so must be eased onto the collar or facing. The stay stitching at neck edge may be used for this purpose.

Use the straight outer muslin collar for the first fitting (see Fig. 69, pp. 111, 112, for complete directions for finished collar).

Match and pin center back of collar to center back of garment. Ease and pin the neck of garment onto the collar to within 1 inch below shoulder seam. Ease collar to neck for one inch, then ease neck to collar to the lapel turn. Repeat for second side and check to make sure the two collar sides match. Baste collar to neck.

A collar basted into place holds the garment in position on the figure when fitting sleeves into the armscye.

PREPARING THE SLEEVE FOR FITTING

Figure 22

a. 1. After the sleeve is cut place a basting down center length grain, the entire sleeve length.
   2. Place basting at cap base from stitching point to stitching point at underarm seams.
   3, 4. Two additional rows of basting above 2, 2 inches apart, if grain is not visible. Baste in any darts at elbow, wrist, or sleeve cap. Baste lengthwise sleeve seam or seams. Leave all the above bastings in the sleeve until it is stitched into armscye.
b. Place ease thread around stitching line of cap, beginning and ending at the center top of sleeve cap, leaving extra length thread ends. Leave underarm seams standing free and *not* basted flat to cap. See Fig. 22.
c. The sleeve cap is at least 1½ inches larger around than the armscye and must be eased into the armscye of the garment by shrinking.
   1. Adjust the sleeve cap over a small press pad or small towel rolled up and folded through the center. Pull up ease thread until the cap curves over press pad, and steam to shrink out the extra ease around cap. This steaming allows the cap to curve over the upper arm into the sleeve without apparent gathers.
d. Shows side view of sleeve cap curve after shrinking.

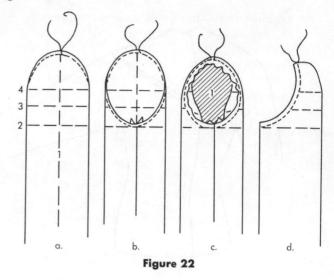

Figure 22

FITTING THE SLEEVES INTO THE ARMSCYE

Figure 23.

The body of the garment should be stitched and steamed with collar basted on and shoulder pads in correct position. It may be placed on the figure or on a dress form and fastened down front for fitting the sleeves.

Both sleeves are fitted along together. Alternate from one to the other to prevent pulling the garment off center to one side.

The notches in the sleeve edge at front and back of cap do not necessarily have to match the corresponding notches on the garment edge, nor do the underarm seams of the sleeve and garment have to match when the sleeve is finally fitted.

The length and cross-grain markings in the sleeve are used in setting the sleeve into the armscye. The length grain *must* be kept *perpendicular* to the floor, while cross-grain markings *must* be kept *parallel* to the floor.

When a sleeve is folded lengthwise through the center with the stitching lines of the underarm seams matching, the back curve of the sleeve cap should be larger than the front cap curve. If this does not exist, difficulties will be encountered when fitting the sleeve into the armscye. It is advisable to superimpose a well-fitting sleeve cap onto the above sleeve and recut the cap before any fitting is done.

The darts and length seams of sleeve are basted only and not stitched until the sleeve has been fitted into the garment.

When fitting in sleeves stand at the side of the model, who should be in front of a mirror.

a. One sleeve is placed into position on the arm, the two ease threads at top are slightly pulled up to ease the cap into position, and the seam edge is tucked under. Adjust the sleeve so that the length grain is perpendicular to the floor, and pin at shoulder-top *x,* the highest point of the shoulder, using a tiny stitch with pin parallel to, and right on, the folded edge of the sleeve. This point falls slightly in front of the shoulder seam.

Adjust the cross grains parallel to floor and pin at widths of chest and back as indicated by *x, x.* Place the forefinger in the garment and the thumb in the sleeve at underarm, bring the two edges together, and pin as indicated by *x.*

Repeat for second sleeve.

Check both sleeves for correct hang, using a weighted string for the length grain; and stand away from the side of the person to check with a rule for cross grain.

b. With the model's arm relaxed, pull up the ease thread and pin down back from shoulder to back width of each sleeve.

With the model's arm slightly eased forward, the fitter sitting down, pin the sleeve on each arm from back width to underarm.

c. With the model's arm relaxed, pull up the ease thread and pin down front sleeve from shoulder to chest width.

Repeat for second sleeve.

With the model's arm slightly held out and away from the body, the *fitter* sitting down, pin each sleeve from the chest width to underarm.

The sleeves should fit into the garment without wrinkles, gathered appearance, or flat stretched section at any point.

If the sleeve does not fit correctly check for *d–l.*

d. Darts at elbow. If one dart, it should fall at elbow bend. Two or more darts should fall equally above and below elbow bend.

e. Gathers at elbow should be distributed equally above and below elbow bend.

f. In a two-piece sleeve, the back seams of the sleeve should be directly opposite each other across the width of the back.

g. If gathers are used, the position of the ends of the gathers at width of back and of chest should be parallel to the floor.

h. If darts are used at sleeve cap, the positions of the two outside darts where sewn into

the garment should be equidistant from the floor.

i. If diagonal wrinkles appear from highest part of the cap, the sleeve cap is too short.

Unpin cap across the shoulder top and let out the top of sleeve cap if the seam allows, and repin sleeve to garment. If wrinkles do not disappear, raise the underarm seam of the sleeve on the armscye of the garment from underarm up toward the width of the chest and of the back. After the adjustment is made, lower sleeve stitching edge under arm and trim away.

j. If diagonal wrinkles appear at upper front and back arm, lift the sleeve cap up with more ease along the armscye of the garment at both front and back.

k. If the underarm of the jacket bends outward toward the arm at under armscye, the garment is too high at underarm. Clip the garment armscye and lower under the arm.

l. If the underarm of the sleeve bends inward toward the body at underarm, the sleeve is too high at this point. Lower by clipping the under armscye of sleeve, then raise on the armscye of the garment.

The girth of the sleeve should be fitted to the arm until a comfortable fit is achieved, or until the sleeve appears correct for the individual.

Since many persons have one arm longer than the other, it is wise to take the length of each sleeve.

A close-fitting sleeve should be fairly long on the hand; whereas a wide sleeve should be shorter.

An estimated long sleeve length for a suit or coat should be halfway between the wrist bend and first thumb knuckle joint. The back edge of the sleeve should reach halfway between the wrist bone and little finger knuckle. This length allows the sleeve to be slightly longer at the back edge. The sleeve length can be adjusted up or down from this measurement.

To measure second sleeve, with the fitted arm and hand straight down, measure from thumb tip to sleeve edge for the front, and from the little finger tip to the sleeve edge for the back edge. Using these measurements, mark second sleeve. This allows each sleeve to fall in the same position across the hands.

BASTING THE SLEEVE INTO THE ARMSCYE

From the right side, baste the sleeve into the armscye, using the slip basting. Turn to the wrong

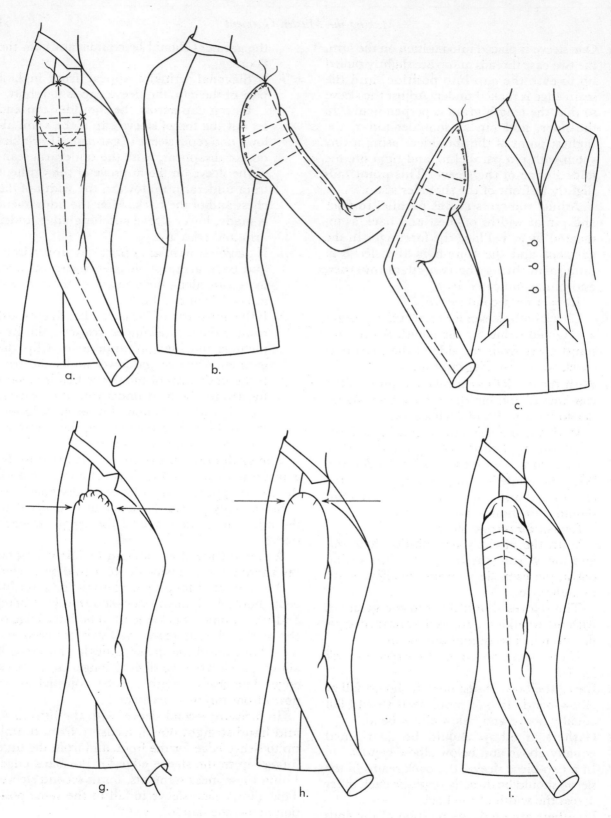

Figure 23

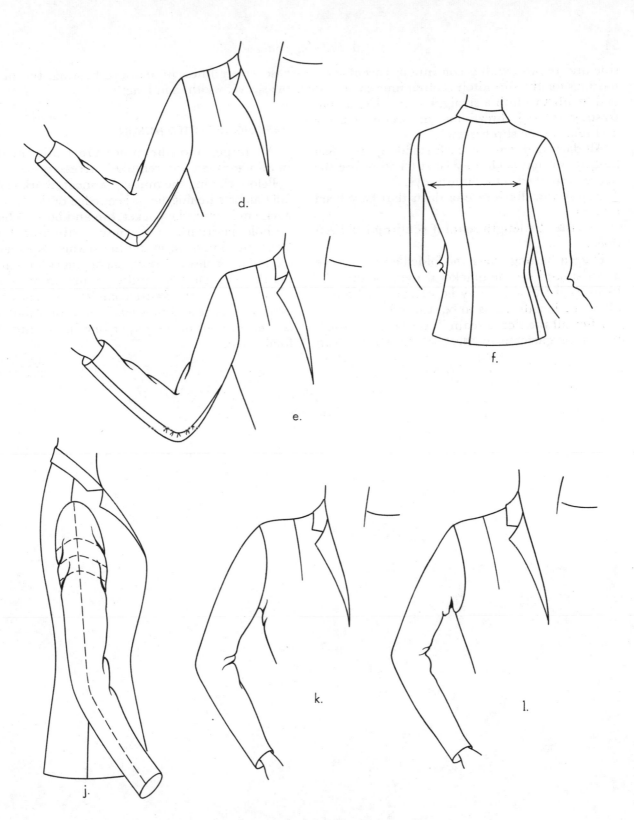

d.

e.

f.

j.

k.

l.

Figure 23 (Continued)

53

side and rebaste with a continuous row of short bastings for the slip stitch is often uneven, and it is difficult to stitch a straight seam. Use a contrasting colored thread for this second basting and remove the slip basting.

All darts and seams are left standing free when basting, so that each may be stitched before the sleeve is stitched into the armscye.

Adjust any elbow ease or darts that have been refitted.

Rebaste the length seam if refitting has been done.

Place a basting along the folded edge of sleeve at wrist, and up the placket if used, so that the turn-up at the wrist may be straightened out to allow the length seams to be stitched.

After all the sleeve seams have been rebasted, try on the garment to check for accuracy of cap ease, straightness of armscye basting, the fit of the sleeve, width, and length.

MARKING THE FITTED MUSLIN

All fitting and alterations are made on the muslin garment and refitted if necessary.

Before ripping the muslin garment, mark carefully along stitching lines, hem edge of sleeve and garment length, the pocket, top and bottom buttonhole positions, and armscye stitching line. Cross markings on matching seams, especially around the armscye, are excellent guides for marking the wool garment and save time in refitting.

When all markings are complete, the garment is ripped apart and pressed. The muslin pattern is used instead of the paper one in cutting the final garment.

General Suggestions in Garment Construction

Tailoring requires the best of one's sewing ability, in accuracy of details, in correct fitting, straight stitching and careful steaming of each step in garment construction. Inaccurate workmanship stands out much more readily in a tailored garment than in a soft wool dress. Uneven or unmatched lapels, poorly pad stitched lapels or collar, poorly made pockets or buttonholes are all noticeable in a tailored garment. A garment will look just as good as the construction processes put into it, and there are no short cuts if one wishes to have a beautiful garment.

Correct foundation: Each fitting should be made over the correct foundation garments to be worn with the article of clothing.

Fit both sides of garment right side out: Since few persons are of identical size on the two sides, each side of the garment should be fitted while on the figure. The center front and back bastings are used as guides to keep the garment centered correctly on the figure.

Shoulder pads: Pads should be adjusted to the correct size and thickness in the first fitting and should be tacked into place, so that in each successive fitting the garment will hang correctly.

Some persons will need to fill out hollows in the figure with padding to create more pleasing results in the outward appearance of the garment. This should be done in the first fitting.

To avoid ripping: Be sure that each part of the garment is correctly fitted and marked before any permanent stitching is done.

Stitch length: Machine stitch length should be the same throughout the garment. Use 15 to 20 stitches per inch, the longer stitch for bulky materials. Length of stitch and tension should be tried on double thickness of scrap material before using on garment.

Stay stitching along all cut edges except length grain of material is necessary in most wool fabrics before basting is done, to prevent edge from stretching out of shape while handling. Use 8 or 10 stitches per inch so that stay stitching will be easy to pull out when no longer needed.

Steaming is most important while constructing a garment. Each seam must be steamed as soon as it is stitched before it is sewed to another section of the garment. The finished garment will need a final steaming.

Cutting the Wool Garment

PLANNING THE WOOL GARMENT LAYOUT FOR CUTTING

The wool garment is not cut until after the muslin jacket or coat has been fitted.

The wool is placed on the cutting table with folded edge along the table edge and cut ends flush with the table ends.

The muslin pattern pieces and the tissue skirt patterns are blocked out on the fabric before any piece is pinned into place. When all pieces are accounted for and in place, check each pattern piece for correct grain, measuring with rule from the folded edge to check length grain, and from the end on the sleeve to check the cross grain with the cap grain. Pin each piece first at grain ends then along the edges to hold securely in place while cutting.

If the fabric has an up and down, as in a pile material, place all pattern pieces on the fabric with the tops facing one end of the fabric.

If the fabric has a stripe, center all center front and center pack pieces either between or on the dominant stripe.

If the fabric has a plaid design, match the plaids both crosswise and lengthwise on the pattern, and center down both front and back.

If the plaid design in the fabric has an up and down or left and right, face all tops of the pattern toward one end of the fabric and match all plaids both crosswise and lengthwise on the pattern.

Chalk any additional seam allowances which are not already included on the pattern. See suggested allowances, p. 38.

In some patterns the under collar is marked to be cut on the length grain at the center back. This collar should be changed so that the collar is cut on the bias, with a seam at center back; otherwise it will be difficult to secure a correct roll of the collar.

Figure 24.

When cutting a skirt with a seam on the inside fold of a pleat, the seam may be transferred from the folded edge of the pleat around to the flat side. This will allow greater smoothness through the hem, for it removes the bulk of the seam away from the fold of the pleat.

Cut out the garment with plain shears.

Mark the garment:

Seam edges with chalk, transfer paper, or tailor tacks.

Darts, tucks, pleats, pockets, buttonholes, and buttons with tailor tacks.

Center front and back with long and short basting.

LINING

The lining of the garment (and interlining if used) should be cut immediately after pattern is removed from the wool in order to allow the same seam and hem allowances as on the garment.

An extra fullness of 3 inches is needed down the center back to allow for ease through the shoulder width. Patterns allow only 2 inches, which is not enough in most instances.

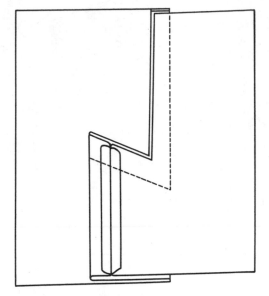

Figure 24

The front lining is cut wide enough to allow ample ease between underarm seam and front facing (of approximately one inch) plus a seam lap along the front facing.

If the garment is on the straight grain and has a seam down the center back, the seam may be folded back and the lining may be cut on the fold, thus eliminating the seam.

Mark all darts and pleats ready for basting after the garment is fitted.

INTERLINING

The interlining is cut exactly as the lining.

Each piece of interlining is spread smoothly on the cutting table and each matching piece of lining is placed on top, with wrong side down. These two matching pieces are then basted all around the edges. The lining is then handled as one piece and basted together for stitching. The fullness, 3 inches at center back, is basted from the neck to the bottom of the garment in a 1½ inch pleat.

CANVAS (OR INTERFACINGS)

Figure 25.

All hymo or wigan used in the construction of a tailored garment must be shrunk. (See shrinking instructions on p. 5.)

Front:

All hymo for fronts is cut identically to the upper part of the front garment, with the center front on the length grain of the canvas.

a. Beginning three inches below the armscye, the canvas curves downward toward the front coat edge to within ½ inch of the front facing edge, where it straightens out to the bottom of the jacket.

A long coat may have the canvas the full front length of the coat. If a soft effect is desired, the canvas may stop just below the bottom button.

b. In the princess style the front section is cut from the front pattern of the garment.

In the side section, the canvas extends 3 inches below the armscye and swings downward in a curve to the front edge of the side section.

Back:

All garments need wigan or light-weight unbleached muslin to reinforce the entire upper back; or, if the fabric is very firm, around the armscye.

This back canvas is always cut on the true bias across the width of back.

c. Begin 3 inches below the armscye and swing an upward arc to the center back, 9 or 10 inches down from the neck edge.

d. For very firm fabric a 3-inch facing is cut from the back armscye pattern, with the width of back on the true bias.

e. For a swing back where the garment flares from the shoulder, the upper back canvas must be cut narrower than the coat back, to fit the wearer. This allows the flare to fall free from the shoulders without causing the garment to slide out on the armscye.

f. The princess is cut into two sections. The center-back section starts 9 or 10 inches below the neck and swings downward to the side seam.

The side-back section starts the same distance from shoulder as its matching seam of front section and swings downward to 3 inches below underarm.

The width of back in each section is on the true bias.

Collar:

g. The canvas for the collar is *always* cut on the bias from the under collar pattern with

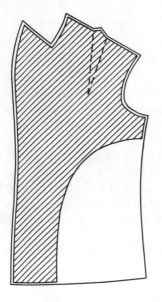

a.

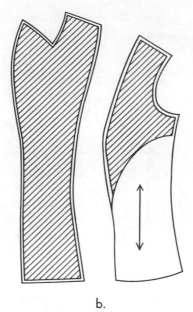

b.

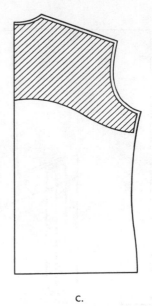

c.

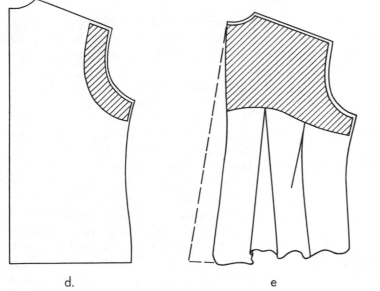

d.

e.

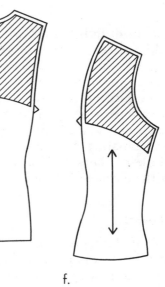

f.

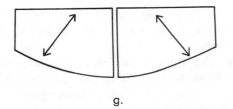

g.

Figure 25

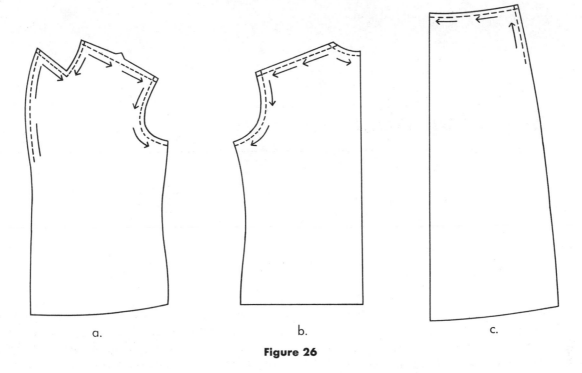

Figure 26

a.   b.   c.

a seam at the center back. The canvas should be cut with material folded so that the canvas grain is correct on the two collar halves as shown in Fig. 69 *b*, pp. 111, 112. Canvas used in the collar is the same as that in the garment fronts.

Bias for sleeve at wrist:

A true bias strip is cut for the lower sleeve edge to give a crispness at sleeve edge. This bias is cut ½ inch wider than the finished hem at sleeve edge and long enough to fit around the lower sleeve, plus seam allowance.

Bias for jacket hem and for some coat hems:

A true bias is cut for the entire circumference of the hem, ½ inch wider than the finished hem of the garment. This is usually of wigan and prevents the hem imprint from showing on the right side of the garment when pressed.

If a crisp or flared effect is desired in a jacket below the waistline, that part of the jacket may be lined with one thickness or more of hymo or crisp canvas. Some styles have additional padding or wadding to give a more flared hipline.

STAY LINE STITCHING BEFORE BASTING

Figure 26.

Fabrics that are loosely woven and have a tendency to stretch or fray should be stitched ⅛ inch outside of stitching line, so that the seam edge is firmly held during construction. Stitch with matching thread, using 6 to 8 stitches per inch.

a, b, c. The following diagrams show positions in which each seam edge should be stitched, and the arrows indicate the direction in which stitching is done.

Do not stitch around corners; cross stitching lines at clear angles on corners.

Both sides of skirt front and back are handled identically.

Steaming Wool

(Figure 1 *a–i*, p. 7, for equipment)

Wool, when steamed, must be handled differently from other fabrics. It should be left slightly damp after steaming, and never pressed thoroughly dry as the fabric will become shiny. One should steam each part of a garment as one progresses with the construction of it.

Use either a steam iron without press cloth or a plain iron with a press cloth. With each, use a moderately warm iron, *never* a hot one. An iron too hot will scorch wool through a press cloth even though the press cloth will show no scorch.

Use heavy drilling or its equivalent for pressing seams, darts, edges, and to shape the garment; and a good quality of cheesecloth for surface steaming. In each, wet one half of the cloth and wring dry; then fold the dry half into the wet half and wring until entire cloth is uniformly damp.

Whenever possible all wool should be steamed with the grain, especially on the surface. The iron must be pressed lightly over the surface. On seams, darts, hems, and seam edges pick up the iron each time you move it and place it down again in the motion of patting the fabric.

Use a long rule along long seams or seam edges, keeping the portion steamed parallel to the rule. This prevents curved seams or edges.

Seams, whether on the surface of the garment or on edges, *must* be steamed open to secure a flat appearance or a sharp turn of a seam because wool cannot be creased open as can cotton. To steam seams open with plain iron, dip the fingers in water and run along the stitching line on the wrong side, moistening *only* the stitching and not surrounding surface. Lightly run the tip of the iron backward between the two seam edges to open seam. Place 3-inch-wide strips of tag or folded wrapping paper between seam and fabric to prevent seam imprint on fabric when steaming. If a steam iron is used, the seam does not need to be dampened.

Where a seam appears at an edge turn, baste the seam along fold turn, slightly rolling seam to the wrong side to prevent stitching edge from showing from the right side. Steam the seam from the wrong side. After the seam is steamed, remove bastings and resteam to remove basting imprints. This is essential as the imprints are difficult to remove if allowed to dry. When imprints are stubborn to remove, they may be steamed along the edge, pounded with a wooden paddle or by hand, then resteamed. Use the paddle also to flatten out bulky spots, such as buttonholes or sharp turns in a seam.

All curved surfaces, such as dart ends, lapel curve, or collar shaping should be steamed over a curved surface. Tailors' hams, press pads, a rolled towel, a padded rolling pin, or anything one can devise may be used. This helps to acquire the correct curve in a garment.

Hem edges, which are fuller than the skirt surface to which they fit, must have the surplus steamed out. Turn hem and baste along folded edge. Mark hem width and trim off surplus. Place an ease thread at hem edge and pull up excess edge to fit skirt with length seams matching. Place tag between hem and skirt and steam by lightly pushing iron from folded edge to seam edge. Steam until the hem lies flat against skirt. The hem width may widen in stretches, so it must be rechecked for width.

Place fabric with a pile on a velvet board and steam darts, tucks, and surface, or, in a plain fabric, use a dry Turkish towel topped with a damp cloth over surface at seam edges and hem. If a velvet board is not available, use two thicknesses of Turkish toweling placed on ironing board, with one thickness of towel over section being steamed. If the pile becomes pressed down, throw steam into section and pound with paddle to raise pile.

Many short seams are difficult to steam on a flat surface but will be easy on a seam board. Sharp turns, such as lapel points, are difficult to turn and steam. Use tailor-trik or sharpened pencil with lead broken off for turning and the point of the seam board for steaming.

When a tailored garment is ready for the lining, a final all-over steaming may be necessary. It is difficult to give some fabrics a sharp steamed edge; therefore, it is advisable to take the finished garment for a final steaming to your favorite dry cleaner who has commercial equipment. The presser should be warned, however, that this is a newly made garment and that special care should be taken in its steaming.

Making the Skirt

BASTING THE SKIRT

If the skirt has pleats, baste and steam the pleats before basting seams.

Pin the marked pleat edge from waist to skirt bottom and baste along folded edge.

Steam the basted fold along a ruled line, remove basting, and resteam to remove basting imprints.

Match folded pleat edge into position, pin and baste fold to skirt the entire skirt length.

If the skirt has a panel or seam front and back, pin and baste the front and back skirt sections before the side seams.

In basting long seams, place the two matching seam edges together flat on a table, with stitching edges matching, and pin together with pins at right angles to cut edge. Baste with the grain, from hem to waistline, to prevent fraying.

Figure 27.

When the front and back sections are basted, spread the two sections flat on the table with side seams matching. Pin front and back sections together along one side seam at points *a, b, c, d,* allowing one half the skirt and one half the ease measurement from center front to center back as planned on the measurement sheet.

  a. waist = ½ waist plus ease
  b. 3 inches below waist = ½ hip plus ease
  c. 6 inches below waist = ½ hip plus ease
  d. widest hip below waist = ½ hip plus ease

Continue pinning the two seams to bottom of skirt.

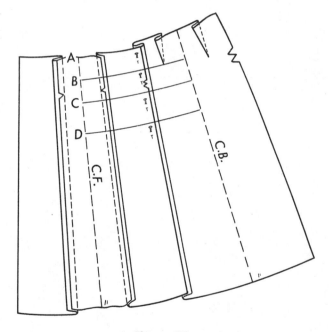

Figure 27

The seam from widest hip to skirt bottom should be the same width as at the widest hip so that the seam may be reduced or increased in width after pinning points *a, b, c, d.* Rule a new basting line from *d* to skirt bottom for basting.

Measure the second side seam from the first, pin, and baste.

From the bottom of placket to waistline put in a guide basting on both front and back placket edge for fitting, exactly matching seams from placket to waist as in the first pinned seam.

Many of the fitting problems will be eliminated if the skirt is basted accurately to the exact size of the waist and hip measurements, plus planned ease.

FITTING THE SKIRT

When making a suit, it is wise to fit the skirt first, then to fit the jacket over the skirt. The lengthwise lines of the jacket and skirt can then be accurately matched, the hip line of the jacket correctly fitted, and the proportions of the entire garment more easily checked.

The skirt *must* be fitted over the foundation garment with which it is to be worn, as foundations vary and may cause refitting problems.

Both sides of skirt are fitted while on the figure as hips vary in size.

BELTS

Figure 28.

There are several methods of finishing a skirt at the waistline, depending upon the desires of the wearer and upon fashions. Whichever method is chosen, the skirt must be fitted onto the belt or its equivalent. Any one of the following methods may be chosen:

a. *Belt can be made entirely of the fabric.* This belt is cut 3 or 4 inches longer than waist measure and twice as wide as the finished belt width, plus the width of seams at ends and sides.

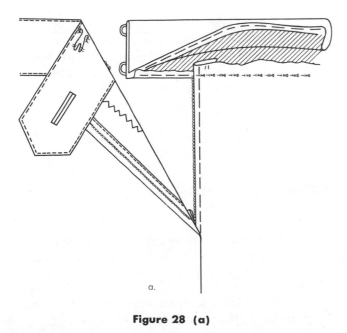

Figure 28 (a)

Turn seams along belt length to wrong side, baste and steam. Fold belt lengthwise through center, allowing outside belt width to be approximately $\frac{1}{16}$ inch wider than under belt width. Baste along fold and steam. Pin the belt around waist of model to the correct tightness, with belt ends at right angles to waist. As the skirt top is inserted between lower belt edges, the lower outer fold of the belt may be turned upward to the upper belt fold so as to be out of the way while pinning the skirt top on the lower edge of the underbelt.

b. *Grosgrain ribbon backing the fabric belt.* Grosgrain is used where fabric is bulky or stretches badly.

Pin the ribbon belt around the waist, with ends at right angles to the figure.

Fit the skirt onto the lower edge of the ribbon as in Process *a.*

Turn the top fabric belt edges to the wrong side, baste, and steam. Pin and baste folded edge along grosgrain ribbon, edge stitch as in 1.

The belt must have two hooks and eyes to fasten the underlap, and may have hooks and eyes or button and buttonhole for the overlap.

c. *Shaped facing in a skirt where skirt top extends above waistline.* This type of waistline finish varies with fashion and must have a stiff inner fitted facing of buckram, horsehair, or the equivalent.

Cut the stiff facing to shape into the waistline at side seams and perhaps center front and center back if the facing is wide, or halfway between center front and side seams or center back and side seams.

Overlap and stitch seams.

Cut a fabric facing to fit the above inner stiffening.

Fit skirt onto the top edge of belting.

Pin fabric facing and baste at top skirt edge, right sides of fabric facing and the three thicknesses stitched together.

Grade seams, trimming inner facing close to stitching line, and turn facing to wrong side of garment.

Sew the two lower edges of facing and belting together.

Outside edge stitching may be used along skirt top.

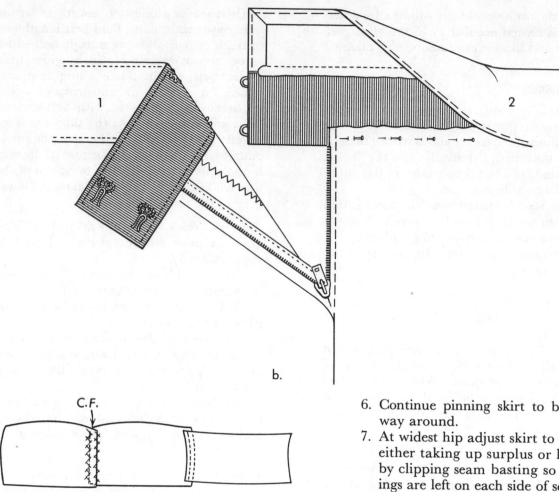

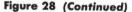

Figure 28 (Continued)

If skirt top has a tendency to roll away from the figure, sew whalebone stays at intervals to the buckram belting and cat-stitch along each side.

1. Adjust the grosgrain belt at waistline, and pin with belt ends at right angles to figure.
2. Place skirt on figure and pin up placket.
3. Pin center front of skirt to belt center and continue pinning to *belt to point below* the bust tip.
4. Pin center back of skirt to belt center and continue pinning to *belt to point below the shoulder* blade.
5. Overlap any surplus skirt at side seams and pin correct tightness at waist or release seams if tight, and pin to correct waist fit.

6. Continue pinning skirt to belt all the way around.
7. At widest hip adjust skirt to correct fit, either taking up surplus or letting out by clipping seam basting so that bastings are left on each side of seam to act as a guide in letting out.
8. Fit side seams from widest hip up to waist by overlapping flat with the front seam edge over the back seam edge.
9. Check with weighted string to see that both seams are perpendicular to floor.
10. Continue fitting skirt from widest hip to skirt bottom, either by letting out or taking up seams, keeping the seams perpendicular to floor.

See the following fitting problems in skirt for further fitting instructions.

FITTING PROBLEMS IN SKIRT

Figure 29.

1 Problem: Side seam swings toward the front. Raise back skirt on belt until side seams hang perpendicular to floor.

2 Problem: Side seam swings toward the back. Raise front skirt on belt until side seams hang perpendicular to floor.

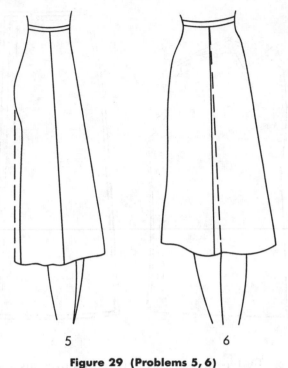

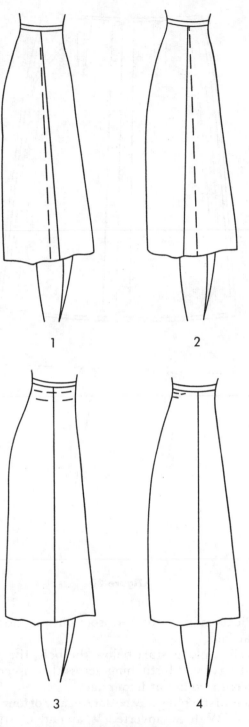

Figure 29 (Problems 1, 2, 3, 4)

3 *Problem:* Entire skirt wrinkles around hips below belt.

   The skirt is too tight. Rip side seams and
   let out until a smooth and easy fit is attained.

4 *Problem:* Back skirt bunches just below back
belt.

Figure 29 (Problems 5, 6)

The skirt is cut too high at center back.
Raise on waistline until wrinkles disappear
and repin to belt.

5 *Problem:* Skirt curls under back hips.

   The skirt is too tight for figure. Let out
   side seams until skirt hangs straight from
   fullest back hips.

6 *Problem:* Center front swings to one side.

   One hip is larger than the other. Raise
   skirt on smaller hip side until center front
   hangs perpendicular to floor.

REBASTING THE SKIRT

Baste across matching belt ends.

Baste along new placket edges.

Baste all refitted seam lines, using slip basting
from the right side and then rebaste on the wrong
side to straighten up any uneven basting lines.
Remove the slip basting.

The skirt on the belt may be handled in either
of two ways:

   1. By tailor tacking skirt and belt about one
   inch apart on the wrong side at lower belt
   edge and cutting apart while finishing skirt
   seams. A colored tailor tack at center front
   and back and at side seams will simplify
   joining skirt to belt. Rebaste belt and skirt
   together and try on for final check before
   stitching.

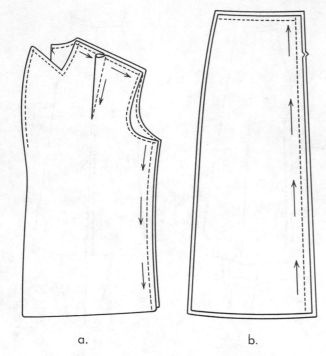
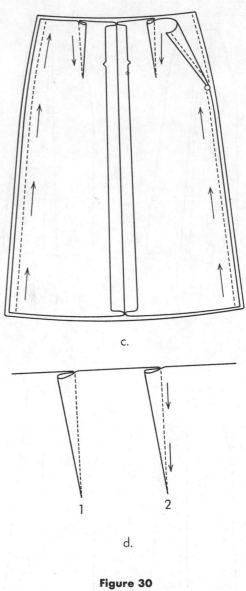

a.   b.   c.

d.

Figure 30

2. By basting skirt to belt between seams and darts and leaving the two basted together while stitching seams.

DIRECTIONS FOR STITCHING DARTS AND SEAMS

Figure 30.

When stitching the garment, it is advisable to stitch with the grain instead of against the grain. This insures a smooth seam and prevents raveling.

A garment that flares around the bottom should be stitched from the bottom up.

a, b, c indicate directions in which seams and darts should be stitched.

d. All darts should be started from the wide or cut edge and stitched to the point.

To insure a smooth flat dart which does not pucker at the point, *do not* stitch as in 1 but follow the folded edge in an inside curve as in 2.

OUTSIDE STITCHING ON PLEATS

Figure 31.

If a skirt pleat extends from belt to skirt bottom on the inside, the pleat edges may be stitched from the inside belt edge to the top of open pleat.

If fabric is bulky, attach a thin, firm lining material at top pleat width at inside and extend to belt edge. This prevents the inside folds of pleat from sagging below the skirt hem.

Pleats may be stitched from outside along the pleat fold.

When pleats start below the belt, the pleats must have width stitching across the top edge to prevent sagging at hem edge.

Width stitching may be done in any of four ways:

a. With an inverted **V** at end of stitched pleat.

b. With a **V** at end of stitched pleat.

c. With horizontal stitching at end of stitched pleat. If a fabric does not take a sharp crease, the stitching may be extended along the folded edge through the hem on the outside.

d. By catching the top width of pleat by hand from the wrong side of skirt; also along the wrong side fold if desired.

e,f. Show the waistline finish outside and inside when a fitted inside belt is used.

ZIPPER PLACKET

Figure 32.

a. The front edge of the zipper placket 1, and the basting along the back of the placket length 2, are continuous lines above the skirt seam 3.

The back or underlap edge of the placket has an extension 4 which is made by folding ⅛ or 3⁄16 inch out toward the seam edge and parallel to basting 2.

This extension is carried ¼ to ½ inch below the lower opening of placket.

Baste and steam the folded edge.

Fold the front or overlap of the placket along the placket edge 1 to the wrong side, baste and steam.

b. If the front placket edge is curved or bias over the hip, reinforce the folded edge in any of the following three ways to prevent curling away from the zipper when fastened.

  1. Run three or four fine, permanent gathering threads through the single thickness of the placket turnback just behind the fold at 1. Pull these threads slightly tighter than the fabric to prevent stretching the placket fold.

  2. On the wrong side of the front placket turnback, place a straight thin tape just touching the fold as at 2, baste into position, and sew by hand along both tape edges.

  3. Cut a straight piece of lining material 1 inch wide along the selvage edge. Place straight cut edge next to the inside fold and baste into place. The placket edge is folded over the lining strip and stitched in with the zipper.

c. 1. Working from the bottom end of the zipper, pin the under extension and baste along the back edge of the zipper very close to the teeth. The zipper pull should escape the belt at the skirt top by ¼ inch.

  2. Turn the skirt wrong side out, place the zipper on machine, fold front placket

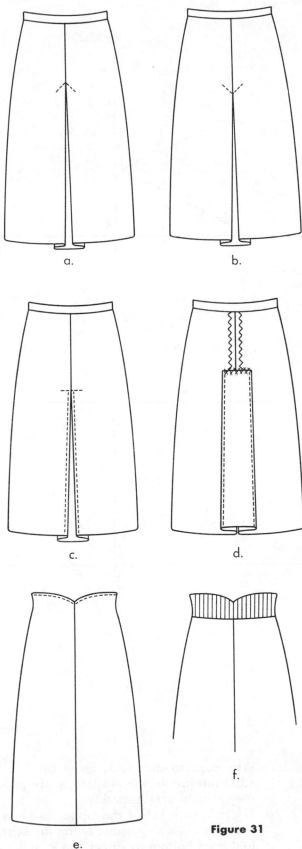

a.

b.

c.

d.

e.

f.

Figure 31

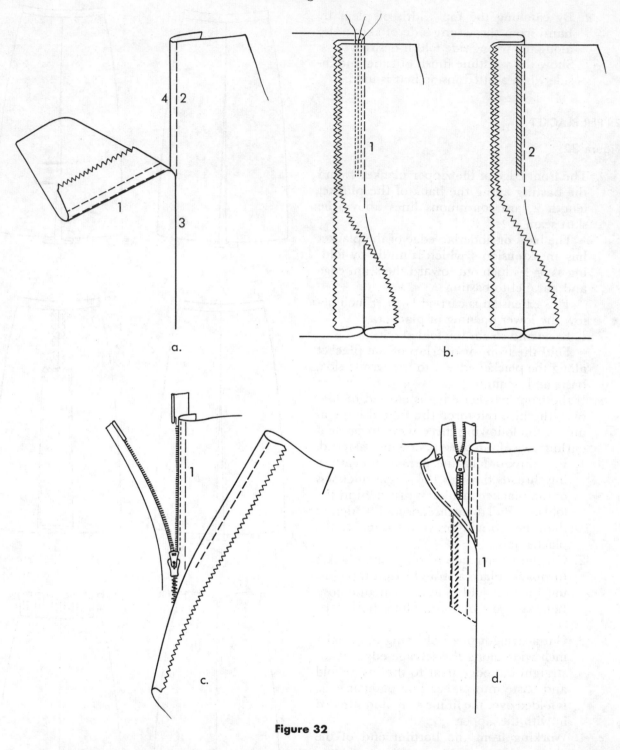

Figure 32

skirt edge to the right, away from the
stitching line of the zipper, before machine stitching is started.
3. Begin ¼ inch below the zipper end and
stitch as close as possible along the skirt
fold from bottom to zipper top as at 1.

d. 1. With the zipper closed, match the two
placket edges of the garment, pin together
and baste the placket closed the full
zipper length.
2. Securely baste the front zipper into position.

3. Place a guide basting parallel to the folded edge of placket and far enough from zipper metal to escape when stitching.

Remove basting, 1, which will open the zipper.

4. Follow the guide basting, stitch the zipper from bottom up to the belt edge.

When stitching along the zipper it is necessary to stop along the length, leave the needle down, and slip the zipper pull to the opposite end out of the stitching path. If the zipper pull is bulky, the stitching may be widened out at the top to allow room for that bulk.

The zipper may be back stitched by hand if preferred. This is done by taking a short stitch through the fabric and zipper, then a very short back stitch for the next forward stitch.

FASTENING THE BELT TO THE SKIRT

(See Fig. 28, pp. 63–64, belt finishes and fastenings)

If the skirt and belt have been tailor-tacked and separated in order to stitch the seams and make the placket, rebaste the two together by matching corresponding tailor tacks.

Stitch the skirt to the under belt from the wrong side along the lower belt edge.

If the skirt belt of the fabric is to have a piped or corded buttonhole, make this buttonhole before stitching the outer belt facing into place. Face the end of the belt receiving the buttonhole with a piece of canvas long enough to receive the buttonhole. (See directions for buttonholes on pp. 78–80.) A corded buttonhole is difficult to make where grosgrain is used but a worked buttonhole is satisfactory.

After the buttonhole is on the right side of the belt end, baste the top belt into place and stitch along the belt edge either by machine or slip stitch by hand.

Finish back side of the buttonhole after the top belt section is basted and stitched into place. See Fig. 43, p. 81, for finish of buttonhole.

The underlap of belt has an extension beyond the zipper up to one inch, with belt ends finished by turning in together before belt is stitched. This end of the belt receives the two eyes of the fastenings.

The top or overlap end of the belt extends up to 1½ inches beyond the outer placket edge on outside of waistline.

The outer belt end may have a squared, pointed, or rounded finish, and is used for the buttonhole end, for snaps, or for hooks and eyes to hold into position.

To locate the hooks, zip up the placket, hold the underextension with eyes into place against wrong side of front belt, and mark for hooks. Sew hooks into place.

With placket zipper and underbelt end hooked, locate overlap fastening position and sew on button, snaps, or hooks and eyes.

SNAPS, HOOKS AND EYES

Figure 33.

Snaps:

In sewing on snaps, sew the thin section of the snap to the overlap of the garment and the heavier section to the underlap.

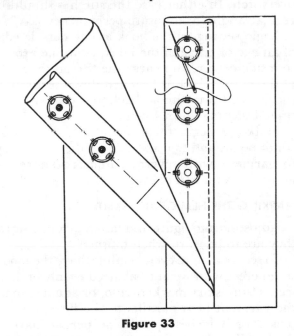

Figure 33

Sew the snap into place with either the buttonhole or overstitch, making the stitches close together and at right angles to the eye of the snap. Carry the thread from eye to eye under the snap to prevent wear on thread by friction between the snap sections when finished.

Figure 34.

Hooks and eyes:

In sewing on hooks and eyes, sew on the fastening with either a buttonhole stitch or plain

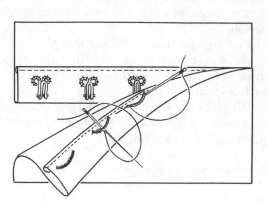
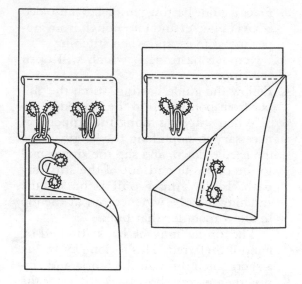

Figure 34

overstitch. In either case the stitches should be regular and tight to insure permanency.

Begin sewing on the hook at one outside edge of an eye or circle of the hook, continue around to inside center, and carry the thread to the tip of the hook, which is fastened down securely to the fabric. Carry thread back to center and continue fastening down second eye.

In the eye, begin stitches at outside eye or circle; continue around to center; catch the inside edge to garment with several stitches; and repeat around second half of eye.

MARKING THE HEM OF THE SKIRT

Adjust skirt to figure and fasten all openings as they are to be worn when finished.

To secure a more even hemline, have the model stand erect with weight balanced evenly on both feet. Using skirt marker, rule, or square, mark the garment hem parallel to the floor, placing pins 2 or 3 inches apart. The person marking the hemline should move around the model, for the model may shift position when turning and cause an uneven hemline.

After hem is marked, fold it to wrong side along marked edge and place pins along fold at right angles to edge, about 2 or 3 inches apart. Pin cut edge up on garment, then try garment on to check accuracy or hang.

Baste the garment hem along the folded edge. Mark hem width parallel to the folded edge and trim the surplus.

If the hem turn-up is wider than garment along which it lies, place an ease thread ¼ inch from the cut edge and pull up until the edge fits smoothly along the garment where it is to be hemmed.

SHRINKING HEM TURN-UP

This surplus ease in hem is shrunk out to eliminate creases or folds from hem fold to hem top.

Place a piece of tag or folded wrapping paper between hem and skirt.

Place a damp cloth over hem, or use a steam iron, and shrink away surplus fullness of hem. Push the iron from fold upward to cut edge to shrink out as much as possible of the surplus ease.

HEM FINISHES

Figure 35.

The hem may be finished in any one of various ways, according to the texture of the fabric.

Stitches in wool hems should be ¼ inch apart, with very tiny stitches taken in the wool, and the thread left easy along the hemming edge.

a. French hem:

If the material is firmly woven and does not fray, the hem edge may be pinked, the seams of the hem matched to the garment seams, and the hem basted to the garment ⅜ inch below the pinked edge.

If the hem has a tendency to fray place two rows of machine stitching ⅛ inch apart along cut edge, the raw edge may be closely overcast, or machine zigzag may be used.

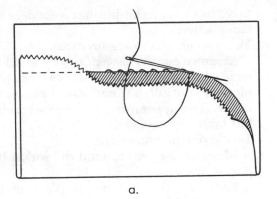

a.

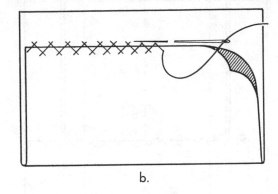

b.

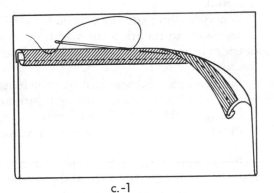

c.-1

c.-2

Figure 35

The loose hem edge (⅜ inch) is folded outward upon the hem itself and held by the thumb while hemmed to the garment at the fold. The hemming stitch actually occurs between the hem and the garment.

When the hem is complete and the ⅜-inch loose edge released, it returns to position flat against the garment.

This hem shows least from the right side and is the easiest to do.

b. Catstitched hem:

After the hem is shrunk, cut the hem edge parallel to the folded edge and baste to the garment with seams matching.

Loosely catstitch over the raw edge. Stitches are ¼ inch apart and ¼ inch down into the hem.

Only one row of stitches shows on right side of the garment.

c. Hem with tape:

Bias silk tape has more elasticity than straight tape; therefore, an inexperienced person will find it easier to apply than straight tape.

The taped hem may be finished by one of two methods:

1. After hem is shrunk, pin bias tape to the cut edge of hem, lying flush with the skirt proper where it is to be hemmed to prevent looseness or folds. Open and fold back tape with right side of tape and garment hem matching. Baste along creases and machine stitch or sew by fine running stitch with sewing silk. Trim seam as narrow as material will allow.

   Fold bias closely over cut edge to wrong side, baste, and stitch along bias edge from the right side.

   Baste the hem to garment, matching seams, and slip stitch or blind stitch to garment.

   This method leaves a narrow binding at top hem edge.

2. The bias or straight tape may be placed wrong side down to right side of skirt hem edge, straddling cut edge. Pin and

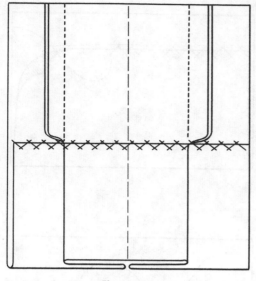

Figure 36

baste to hem edge. Stitch tape to skirt hem from right side of tape along lower edge.

Pin upper edge of tape to garment with seams matching, baste, and slip stitch or blind stitch.

Figure 36.

Seam in pleat:

When a seam appears at the under side fold of a pleat, the seam is clipped to the stitching line just above the hem edge to allow the seam within the hem to be pressed wide open.

PLEATED SKIRT

A full pleated skirt is cut on the length grain with each end of the fabric torn or cut along a drawn thread.

Measure the finished skirt length at side hip, plus hem at bottom and seam at top. Any one of three measurements may be used, depending on the amount of material on the inside pleat depth. However, the wider inside pleat has a tendency to give a more pleasing effect as well as not to lose its effectiveness as quickly as the narrower pleat depth.

Figure 37.

Pleating:

a. Three to one measurement.

Measure *three times* around the widest hip, plus seams. This "three to one" pleated skirt

takes more material but has a tendency to hang better.

b. Two and one-half measurement.

Measure *two and one-half times* around the widest hip, plus seams. This skirt has wide pleats on outside but narrower ones on the inside. The appearance is the same as in *a* but takes less material.

c. Two to one measurement.

Measure *two times* around the widest hip, plus seams.

Because of the very shallow pleats underneath, this skirt does not hold the pleats as well as *a* or *b*, but does require much less material.

When sending the skirt to be pleated, it is necessary to mention the width of pleats outside; also whether the pleating is 3 to 1, 2½ to 1, or 2 to 1.

Baste, stitch, and seam all but one length seam. Turn hem, baste, hem by hand, and steam. (See Fig. 35, p. 71 for hems.)

Pleats may all go one direction around figure.

Pleats may form a box pleat at center front, turn in opposite direction, and form an inverted pleat at center back. This method requires a center front basting down skirt length (which should be on the surface of the fabric) and *never* down a seam, which would spoil the appearance of the skirt.

Send the skirt to a professional shop to be pleated.

d. Fittings.

Put row of basting along waist edge and around the widest hip position, basting all pleats flat.

Place belt around waist with placket opening at side or center back. (For placket openings see Fig. 28 *a, b,* pp. 63–64.)

Place skirt around figure, hold in place, and put tape line around widest hips to hold pleats temporarily to the figure until skirt is anchored to the belt.

Adjust length and hem evenness by raising or lowering skirt under tape at hip.

Smooth front pleats up from widest hip to waist and pin to belt.

Smooth back pleats up from hip to waist and pin to belt.

Smooth side pleats up from hip to waist and pin to belt.

Remove basting at waistline.

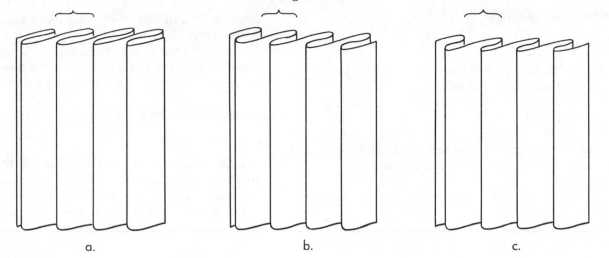

a.   b.   c.

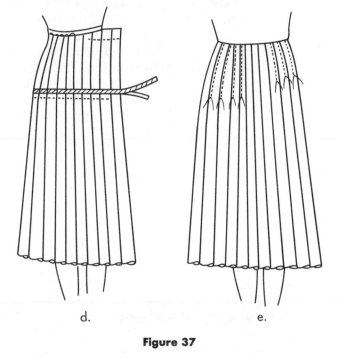

d.   e.

Figure 37

Each outside pleat edge must be perpendicular to floor. This is achieved by smoothing each pleat from hip up to waist and pinning to belt. The pleat edges on the outside will then fall closer together as they approach the waist.

When each pleat is adjusted at the waist, remove the tape from hip and pin each pleat from hip to the waist. Some pleats will overlap more than others because of body curves. Check the hem line to see that it is parallel to the floor.

Remove skirt from the figure.

Baste skirt at lower belt edge.

Baste securely each pleat edge from widest hip up to belt edge, basting the pleat edge *only* through one thickness of the skirt and not through the underneath pleats. Steam pleats from wrong side of skirt as new pleat edges are formed.

Rip back the hem at open seam edges and baste the open seam from hem edge to placket end of skirt.

Stitch and steam open the seam.

Rebaste the hem across seam and hem by hand.

Steam pleats from waist to widest hip and leave free from waist to skirt bottom if desired.

e. Stitch pleats.

Pleats may be edge stitched from waist to desired depth.

Measure down from waistline the desired depth of stitching and baste around the hip so as to keep each pleat stitching the exact length desired.

1. As shown on the left-hand side.

Stitch along the exact edge of the outside pleat edge and leave long threads at hip end of pleat. Pull threads to wrong side, thread both threads into needle, and fasten securely by hand.

2. Stitch back from outside pleat edge the desired width and diagonally out to pleat edge at hip end of stitching. Pull both threads to wrong side, thread into needle, and fasten securely by hand.

Remove all basting and resteam.

Placket finish, Fig. 32, p. 68.

Belt finish, Fig. 28 *a, b,* pp. 63–64.

INSIDE SEAM FINISHES

Figure 38.

The edge finish of inside seams will depend upon the firmness of the fabric.

If the seam is covered with a lining, no edge finish is needed.

All inside seams *must* be cut parallel to the stitching line, regardless of the seam width or its location. Any of the following finishes may be used:

a. 1. Pinking is the simplest and most satisfactory method.
　　2. Machine stitching and pinking give the edge a firmer finish than pinking alone, especially where fabric is likely to stretch or fray.
b. Blanket stitch may be used on a fabric that has a tendency to fray. For some persons it is easier to do than overcasting.
c. 1. Overcasting is made by taking stitches ⅛ to ¼ inch apart and the same depth into the seam edge.
　　2. First edge stitch ⅛ to ¼ inch from cut edge, and overcast around stitching.
d. Bound seams add thickness to seam edges and should be used only on material that

frays badly and where no other finish seems satisfactory.
e. A machine attachment zigzagger or a machine which does edging is very satisfactory for seams which have a tendency to fray.

SEAM FINISHES ON RIGHT SIDE OF GARMENT

Figure 39.

a. Double stitched seam: This seam is first stitched on the wrong side, and edges are steamed wide open. From the right side, stitch two rows of stitching equal distance from seam, one on either side.
b. Welt seam: This seam is used in polo coats or as a decorative seam on tailored garments.

　　The seam is stitched first on the wrong side.

　　One seam edge is trimmed away to the width of the finished seam on the right side.

　　The two seam edges are pressed to one side with the wider seam uppermost. From the right side, place a guide basting parallel to stitching line, the width of the narrow cut seam underneath. From the right side, stitch along basting, avoiding the narrower seam width.

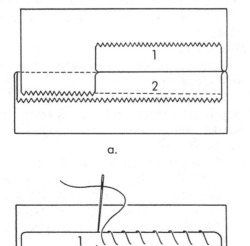

a.

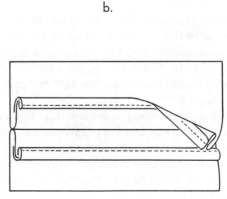

b.

c.

d.

Figure 38

c. Double stitched welt: This seam is used on a polo coat or as a decorative seam on tailored garments.

The seam is stitched first on the wrong side.

One seam is trimmed down to the width of the finished seam on the right side.

The two seam edges are pressed to one side with wide seam uppermost.

From the right side a guide basting is made parallel to stitched seam, just escaping the narrow underneath seam.

Machine stitch along basting, also along the first stitched seam edge.

d. Edge stitched or corded seam: This seam is used where outside stitching is used to accent the seam.

The seam is basted and stitched on the wrong side of the garment.

The two edges are pressed together toward the center back or center front of the garment and basted into position. From the right side the seam is stitched very close to the folded seam line.

e. Plain seam: This is the most commonly used of all seams. The seam is stitched on the wrong side; the edges are trimmed parallel to stitching line and pressed wide open.

f. Slot seam: This is a decorative seam, where two folded seam edges come together and are stitched on a matching or contrasting strip of material.

A straight or shaped strip of fabric is cut, and a basting is placed down its length center.

The seam allowance of each garment edge is folded to wrong side, basted, and steamed.

The two steamed edges are matched along the basting line of the strip and basted into position.

Top stitching is done at equal distances from the folded edge.

g. Strap seam: A method of decorating a plain seam, but rarely used.

The seam is first stitched on the wrong side, edges are trimmed parallel to stitching line, and steamed wide open.

A strip of cloth covers the outside of seam.

This strip is cut desired width plus seams on each side.

Seam edges are turned to wrong side, basted, and steamed.

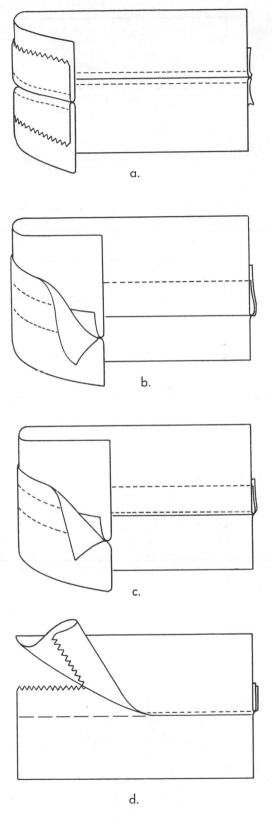

a.

b.

c.

d.

Figure 39

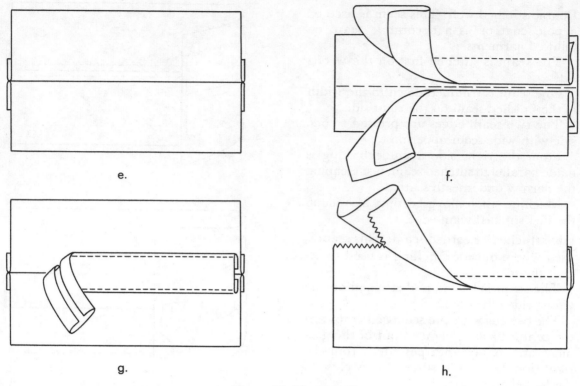

e.

f.

g.

h.

Figure 39 (Continued)

The strip is pinned and basted over stitched seam, and edge is stitched.

h. Tuck seam: This seam has one row of stitching on the outside from the folded edge.

Fold back the overlapping seam along the stitching line, baste, and steam.

Match the folded edge to the stitching line of its matching seam, baste, and stitch parallel to the folded edge, seam width uppermost.

From the right side, place a guide basting parallel to the stitching line, the exact width of the desired seam and escaping trimmed seam underneath.

Machine stitch along the guide basting or pick stitch by hand.

Fasteners on Garments

Usually a tailored garment is buttoned if fastenings are used, but a zipper or fly front may be used.

Sometimes in commercial patterns the spaces between buttonholes are not accurate, or one may wish to shift the buttonholes either up or down, or change the number indicated on the pattern. To be sure of accuracy, mark the top and bottom positions of buttonholes on the garment and then accurately divide and mark between these two marks for the desired number of buttonholes. If the buttonholes end at the waist or continue below, place a buttonhole at the low waistline to add apparent length to the figure.

In women's garments the right side carries the buttonholes and overlaps onto the left, which holds the buttons.

The end of the buttonhole should extend slightly over the center front line toward the garment edge. This extension should be one half the width of the shank of the button when sewn to the garment, which is approximately 1/16 of an inch.

Figure 40.

To be accurate in spacing the buttonholes, make a ladder, using long and short bastings.

a. The center front basting is already in the garment.

b. Toward the cut edge from the center front place a basting for one end of the buttonhole one half the button shank width from the center front basting.

c. On the garment side place a basting the exact length of the buttonhole.

d. Place cross bastings for each buttonhole position.

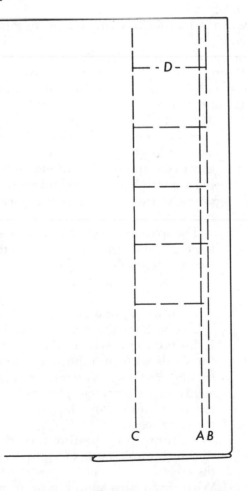

Figure 40

77

These markings are placed on the right side for worked and corded buttonholes, and on the canvas side for piped buttonholes.

In all garments opening down the center front, sew the button along the center front grain line, which is already marked with a basting.

To secure the correct position for buttons, pin the right and left garment edges together and mark accurately each button position through the buttonholes on the right garment section to the left garment section along the center front basting.

In wool use canvas between the two thicknesses of material to prevent the buttonhole from pulling away from the fabric.

CORDED BUTTONHOLE

Figure 41.

This buttonhole is used more frequently than any other on tailored garments and is the simplest to make.

Make ladder for buttonholes on the right side of garment.

Cut a true bias of fabric 2 inches wide and 1 inch longer than the buttonhole. Mark center length with basting. Cut two lengths of twine the length of the bias.

a. 1. Along the side of the center basting with cord to wrong side of material, baste the material tightly around the cord, using short running stitches of matching sewing thread. Sew the second cord on the opposite side of the basting parallel to first cord.

The space between stitchings that hold the cord determines the width of the finished buttonhole.

This space should be less than ¼ inch as a buttonhole when finished should *never* be wider than ¼ inch.

To check for this width, hold the material taut, crosswise of the cords, push the cords with thumbnail to the center basting. *The two cords should touch.* If there is any space between, the cords are too far apart; if they overlap, the cords are too close together.

2. With contrasting basting thread, mark the buttonhole ends at right angles to the cords.

b. With raw seams standing up from garment, place the corded section on marked buttonhole of garment, matching center basting to marked buttonhole, and contrasting bastings at ends on buttonhole section to ends of buttonhole on the garment.

Pin and baste into position between the cords.

Stitch the corded section to garment exactly on basting along cord and stitch each end of stitching back on itself to prevent ripping, or leave a long thread on each end of the stitching line so that the two stitching ends may be checked for correct length. Either lengthen or shorten, if necessary; thread loose threads in needle, and fasten securely.

Check on the canvas side of garment to see that the two stitchings are exactly parallel and that the ends of stitchings are opposite each other.

c. Spread the two raw edges and cut through length of buttonhole between cords to within ³⁄₁₆ inch from end, then diagonally out to stitching ends.

d. Pull the seams of buttonhole through to wrong side and from the right side baste the corded edges together.

e. With buttonhole facing the machine, and the garment folded back, locate the triangle, and stitch securely in an arc to the seam at end of the buttonhole. Repeat for second end.

To eliminate bulk at ends, cut away any excess cord from buttonhole, also some of the pleat formed around cord.

Steam buttonhole. If fabric is bulky, pound with paddle while steaming to flatten out buttonhole.

PIPED BUTTONHOLES

Figure 42.

In making piped buttonholes place the ladder marking on the *canvas* side of the garment. (Fig. 40, p. 77.)

The material for piping may be cut either on the straight grain or on the true bias.

Cut piping pieces 1½ inch wide times the buttonhole length plus ½ inch for seams, and baste each strip through the length center.

Baste the center grain of piping to buttonhole length with right sides of fabric facing.

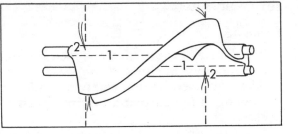

a.

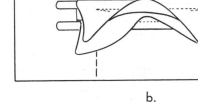

b.

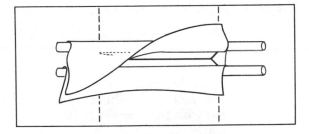

c.

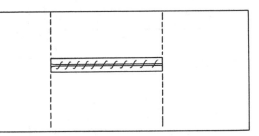

d.

e.

Figure 41

a. From the canvas side of garment stitch a rectangle the exact length of the buttonhole and about ³⁄₁₆ inch wide. Machine stitch should be short to secure stitching.

Begin stitching at the center of a long side, stitch to the end, leaving the needle down to use as a pivot while turning a corner. Continue stitching the entire buttonhole, overlapping the first three or four stitches.

Count the stitches across the end to insure a more accurate width in all buttonholes.

b. Cut the buttonhole through the center to within ³⁄₁₆ inch from the ends, then cut diagonally out to the corners.

c. Pull the fabric through to wrong side.

d. Press all seams around buttonhole away from the opening.

e. From the right side fold the facing, forming a piping ½ the width of the buttonhole opening and baste along fold. Repeat for second side.

f. Baste folded piped edges together down center of buttonhole.

g. Turn garment to wrong side, place buttonhole in position, and stitch the triangle to the piping in a slight arc. Stitch the facing along buttonhole length to the seams by machine, or back stitch by hand.

Trim away any excess material, leaving up to ¼ inch seam around buttonhole.

Steam buttonhole, remove basting, and resteam.

If the buttonhole seems thick, pound with paddle while steaming.

Make the facing for the piped buttonhole the same as for a corded buttonhole.

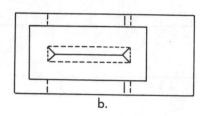

a.

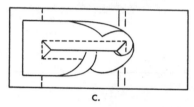

b.

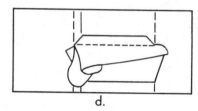

c.

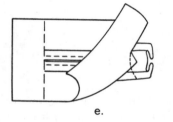

d.

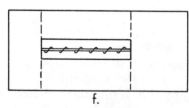

e.

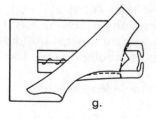

f.

g.

Figure 42

BUTTONHOLE FACING

Figure 43.

The facing of the corded or piped buttonhole may be finished in either of two ways.

After the several buttonholes are made, adjust the facing of the garment, pin into permanent position.

From the right side of the garment mark with pins through on the facing the length of each buttonhole, then carefully baste each buttonhole on the wrong side of the facing.

   a. This method produces a neat bound buttonhole in the facing. Cut true bias facings from lining silk 1 inch wide and ½ inch longer than buttonhole to be faced.

     1. Cover each buttonhole length on the facing with the bias silk, with right sides of materials together.

       Stitch from the facing side a rectangle around marked buttonhole, the exact size of buttonhole to be faced.

       Cut through the buttonhole length to within ³⁄₁₆ inch of ends, then diagonally out to corners.

     2. Pull bias through the rectangular opening to wrong side of the garment, fold along stitching line, baste, and steam.

     3. This opening is fitted to the wrong side of the buttonhole, basted, and closely slip stitched into position.

       This method is simple to make with no frayed edges around the facing side of the buttonhole, also the buttonhole is reversible.

   b. This method, though apparently simpler, is not as satisfactory as Method *a.*

     1. Match the facing to buttonhole, locate the exact position of the facing, and stitch a rectangle on facing the exact size of the buttonhole proper.

       Baste the facing of the garment permanently into position. Baste around each buttonhole so that facing and garment will not slip.

       Cut the facing through the buttonhole to ³⁄₁₆ inch to the end, then diagonally out to the four corners. The stitching forms a stay around edge which is to face the buttonhole.

     2. Turn the facing seams to the wrong side around the buttonhole.

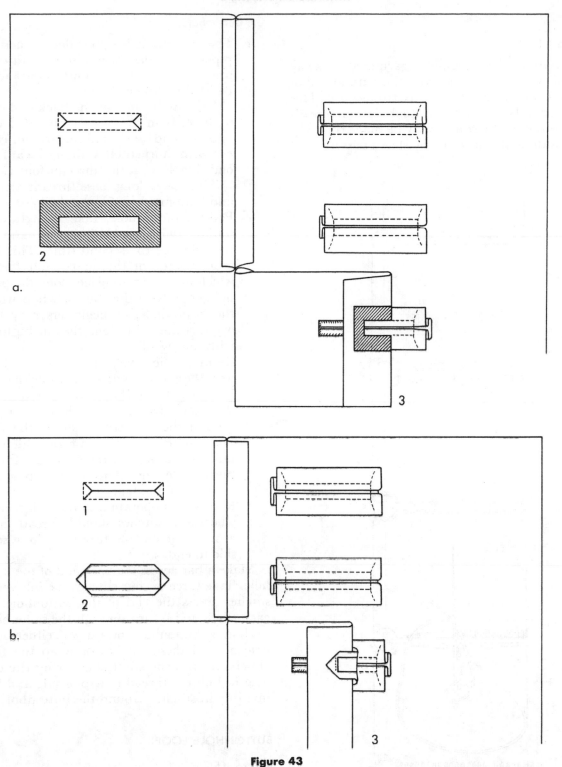

Figure 43

3. Baste and closely slip stitch to the back side of the buttonhole.

This method is likely to leave frayed ends of fabric at turned edge and is more difficult to handle than Method *a*.

The piped or corded buttonholes should be made through the outer fabric and the canvas, while the worked buttonhole is made through the outer garment, the canvas, and the facing and should always be made by hand.

A Tailoring Manual

WORKED BUTTONHOLE

Figure 44.

In buttonholes on tailored garments cut away a small section of fabric from the outside end of the buttonhole to hold the button shank. This enlarged end prevents the buttonhole from spreading around the button. It may be made by a regular buttonhole cutter or by sharp scissors.

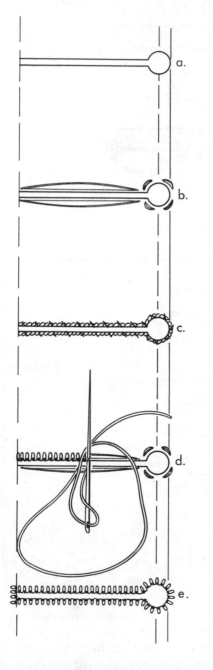

Figure 44

Cut buttonhole:

a. The buttonhole length is determined as for piped or corded buttonholes, and cutting must be straight. The buttonholes may be padded in either of two ways:

b. Take a small stitch at the back end of buttonhole, then at the beginning of eye at opposite end, and continue around cut-out eye with short stitches; then repeat for second side. Repeat this three or four times.

This leaves long loose threads along top and bottom edge of buttonhole, or

c. Pad the buttonhole. Take a length of buttonhole twist, double in center, and twist; then double the second time. This leaves four strands of thread twisted together, which are held into place along the buttonhole edge with the thumb when working the buttonhole, or beginners may lightly overcast the twist along the cut buttonhole with sewing silk.

d. Begin at the lower right-hand end away from the garment edge, and fasten the thread invisibly. Place the needle down through the open edge, up through the fabric, and around the pad stitch; swing the thread under needle point from right to left, then pull the needle at straight angles from the buttonhole edge. This leaves a purl at the cut edge of the hole.

e. Repeat this operation to the enlarged end, where the stitches should spread fanwise around the end. Buttonhole along second side to end.

Make a bar across the back end of the buttonhole. Take three or four stitches the full width of stitches across the end of the buttonhole. Take each stitch and return through the same hole.

Holding buttonhole toward you, either buttonhole around these stitches or wrap the thread closely around the stitches covering the entire length. Pull the thread to wrong side and fasten invisibly in stitches around the buttonhole.

BUTTONHOLE LOOPS

Figure 45.

Loops may be used in place of buttonholes.
a. Cut a true bias strip 1 inch wide and long enough to make several loops.
b. Fold lengthwise through the center with right side in and machine stitch parallel to

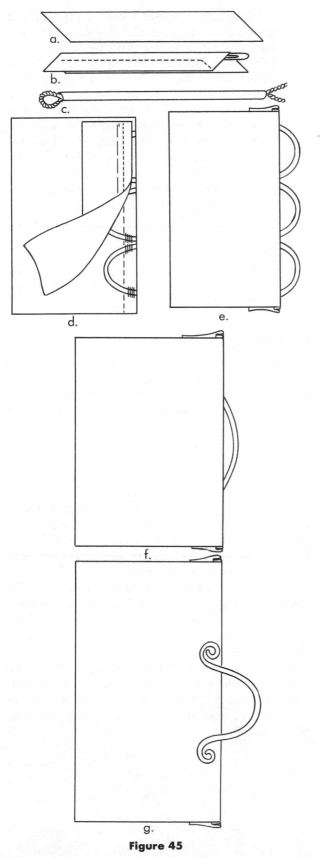

Figure 45

folded edge the desired width of finished loop. Widen out one stitching end on the bias through which to start the turning of bias right side out. Stretch the bias while stitching to prevent stitching from breaking while turning.

Trim bias seam the same width as the tube.

To turn the bias, insert a bodkin into the enlarged bias end and sew bias to bodkin eye. Push the bodkin through the tube and turn tube right side out.

c. Thread a wool yarn through the bodkin and pull through the tube. This straight yarn pads the loop and also prevents the tube from stretching.

d. Measure a loop long enough to allow a button to slip through, plus seam at each end. All other loops are cut from this first pattern loop.

Mark the correct buttonhole positions along the seam edge.

Place a loop, seam side up, in a U-shaped position around each buttonhole position, with stitching lines of loops and garment matching, and with the loops lying back on the garment. Baste loops securely to garment.

Place facing into position covering loops at garment edge, pin, baste, and stitch; then remove all bastings.

e. Fold facing to wrong side allowing loops to extend out from the seam edge.

f. Loops may lie flat along the garment edge when used to hold up an under lap of a wrap-around coat, or when an inconspicuous loop is desired.

g. A loop may be used at garment edge as a decorative fastening.

SEWING ON GARMENT FASTENINGS

Figure 46.

The thread used in sewing on buttons should be of heavy linen which is already waxed, or of buttonhole twist, which should be waxed.

If a backing button is not used the button is sewed only through the outer fabric and canvas.

a. Buttons showing different arrangement of stitches.

b. On all garments buttons should be sewed on with a shank. This shank length should be the thickness of the material surrounding the shank.

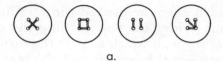

a.

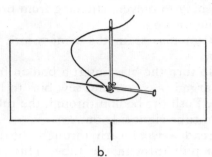

b.

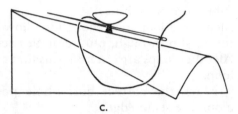

c.

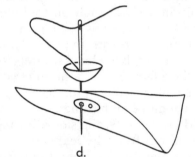

d.

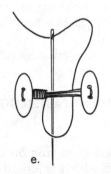

e.

Figure 46

To secure this shank hold a pin, nail, or an equivalent over the button's eye and pass the stitches over this object.

c. When the button is sewed on, remove the object, pull the button to the loop ends, and with the needle and thread between the button and cloth, wind the thread several times around the shank to hold the button away from the garment. Pull the thread to the wrong side and fasten firmly to the canvas.

d. In a heavy coat where strain on the garment is great, use a small backing button on the facing side of the garment. Sew the thread through the eyes of both the top and the backing button.

e. Sewing buttons together, using a shank. This button arrangement is used where two edges touch without overlapping.

DOUBLE-BREASTED GARMENTS

Double-breasted garments may have two rows of buttons and buttonholes, two rows of buttons and one row of buttonholes, one row each of buttons and buttonholes, or just an overlap, held in place by a belt.

In the long double-breasted coat, the under extension, if not buttoned, should be held in place by a tie made of the lining, or of matching grosgrain ribbon about 1 inch wide.

Cut two strips of lining on the length grain 15 inches long and 2½ inches wide. Fold each strip lengthwise through the center with right side in, baste, and stitch down length and across one end. Turn right side out and steam.

After basting the body of the lining to the armscye sew the two raw ends of the ties securely into the *right armscye* at underarm seam along with the lining. When the sleeve lining is put in, the raw seams are hidden.

On the underlap of the coat at the waistline position, make a loop at garment edge through which one tie is slipped and tied to second one to hold up the underlap of the garment (see Fig. 45, p. 83).

Making the Jacket or Coat

PREPARING INSIDE CUTS ON GARMENT SURFACE

Figure 47.

Reinforced corners or turns:

Any seam cut at any angle within the surface of the fabric must be reinforced before stitching to prevent the turn of the cut from fraying.

a. Place a basting thread along the stitching lines of the two intersecting seams.

b. Cover the point of intersection with a 1- to 2-inch square of silk crepe or light-weight lining fabric with right sides facing and with grains matching, and baste into place.

c. From the seam edge, stitch an arrowhead to the point of seam, pivot the fabric around the needle, take one short stitch across the point and stitch back to seam edge as shown by dotted lines. Clip from seam edge as shown by solid line to point, but not through stitching.

d. Turn along basted stitching line to wrong side, baste and steam seam to the wrong side. The lining square will form folds. Cut off surplus square, leaving ample seam. This forms a seam around inside cut with no frayed edges at seam turn.

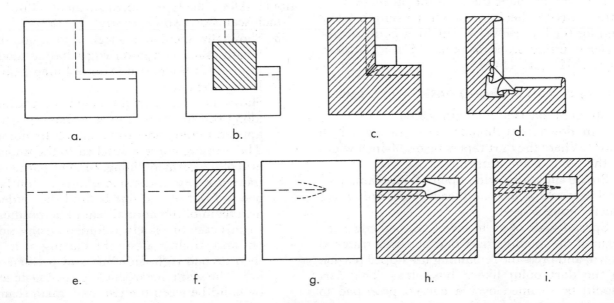

a.   b.   c.   d.

e.   f.   g.   h.   i.

Figure 47

e. When a garment is cut straight in from an edge, the seam end may be reinforced to strengthen it, especially if a pocket, godet, or other trim is to be used.

f. Place 1-inch square over cut end.

g. Beginning ¾ inch from cut end, stitch an arrow point around cut end as indicated by dotted lines and clip to stitched end, but not through the stitching.

h. Turn end seam to wrong side ready for needed finish.

i. Place a silk square on wrong side of fabric and stitch from the right side, using the silk only as a reinforcement.

BASTING THE GARMENT

The jacket or coat is basted together as in the muslin garment after stay stitching is done.

Use heavy-duty thread in contrasting color, and short, firm basting stitches where strain appears.

All plaids, checks, and stripes must be matched crosswise and lengthwise.

All inside cuts must be reinforced to prevent fraying at cut turn.

Use the same directions which have been used for the muslin for fitting the wool garment.

FITTING THE WOOL GARMENT

Because muslin and wool fabric handle somewhat differently, it will be necessary to check carefully the fit of the wool garment before doing any stitching lest there may be some slight refitting problems.

It is wise to check the fit of the jacket over the fitted skirt to check for matching length seams and for the hip size before stitching permanently. Refer to fitting problems under Muslin Garment, Figs. 20–23, pp. 41–54.

STITCHING AND STEAMING DARTS AND SEAMS

Stitch all darts and length seams.

Trim down front shoulder dart, leaving ⅜-inch seam. Where the dart tapers below ⅜-inch width to the point, leave untrimmed.

Steam all seams wide open. Trim seams parallel to stitching line, and leave edges unfinished where lining is used.

Spread wide open to lower clipped edge, the seam of the shoulder dart that has been trimmed down, and press the remaining unclipped portion to the dart point like a box pleat. This dart should be steamed over a curved press pad to secure a good curve at the dart end.

From the wrong side, steam all uncut waist, shoulder, and neck darts toward the center front and center back.

Steam all darts and curves over curved press pad for best results.

Tailor tack the shoulder seam (except where a shawl collar is used) with tacks 1 inch apart from neck to armscye edge and clip apart. These tacks allow the seam to be rebasted exactly as in the original fitting.

BASTING THE LINING

At the end of the final fitting of the jacket or coat and before the garment seams are trimmed, baste the lining for stitching.

Since the lining must fit exactly into the jacket or coat, make the same alterations as in the garment.

Mark on the lining the same permanent stitching lines, darts, etc., as appear on the finally fitted garment before garment seams are trimmed.

Baste the lining, except the sleeves, which may be stitched at any time before being attached to inside of garment.

Baste the 1½-inch pleat (3 inches out flat) down the back length.

A dress shield may be cut and basted into the underarm seam if desired.

LINING SHIELD PATTERN

Figure 48.

The outline of the shield is drawn the exact size used for a shield in a lined garment, allowing ⅜-inch seams on two lower straight edges.

a. Shows the shield folded right side out on the length grain with lower edges basted ready to insert at underarm seam of lining before lining is stitched.

b. Shows the shield with the length grain falling along the stitching line after having been applied to the underarm seam of the lining. The armscye curve is stitched to the underarm of the garment lining. In some garments there are two underarm seams which fall one in front of and one behind the underarm seam of the normal seam line position. In this case the shield is folded wrong side out and stitched along the basting as in a, then turned right side out and pressed as in b. The seam line of shield is then fastened by hand between the two underarm seams of the garment lining.

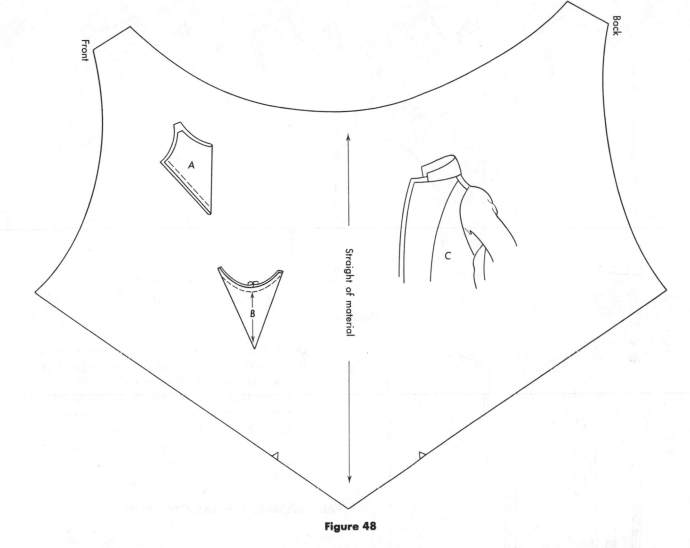

Figure 48

c. Shows the finished appearance of the shield in the lined garment with the two bias edges left free.

STITCHING THE CANVAS DARTS AND SEAMS

Figure 49.

After the garment is fitted the hymo darts or seams are stitched exactly the size of the garment, for the canvas and front must fit together perfectly.

a. In the hymo, cut away all the dart along the stitching line.

b. Cut a strip of hymo the length of the darts and 1 inch wide along the length grain.

Match the two cut edges of dart to the center of strip, pin, and baste into position.

c. By machine, zigzag stitch across the dart, sewing edges securely to the strip.

Steam over curved board for smooth end finish.

d. When a princess line is used, the two princess stitching seams of the canvas are matched by overlapping.

The same seam allowance is used as in the garment.

Stitch two parallel rows of machine stitching ¼ inch apart along the seam and cut away excess seam.

BASTING THE CANVAS TO THE GARMENT

Figure 50.

Place the garment right side down on the table.

Smooth the canvas fronts on garment fronts, matching seams or darts, and pin into position.

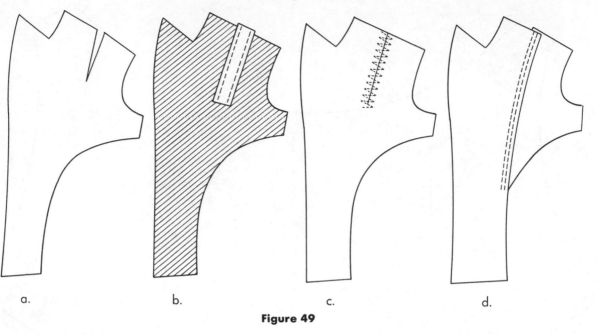

Figure 49

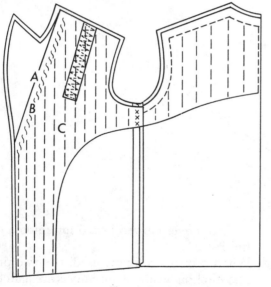

Figure 50

the full width of the front canvas, so that the canvas and garment fronts are held together without wrinkles in either one.

Leave the section from diagonal basting to the lapel point free for pad stitching.

Baste back canvas to upper back, first down center back, across neck and shoulder, and down around armscyes 1½ inches from cut edge.

PAD STITCHING THE GARMENT FRONTS

Figure 51.

The pad stitch is used to fasten the canvas into the garment and at the same time to shape and roll the lapels of the garment and the collar.

The pad stitch is made by pushing the needle through the canvas, catching a few yarns of wool, and returning the needle to the canvas side, all in one stitch process. (For best results use No. 10 needle and matching sewing thread.) The stitches are ¼ inch across, with ¼ inch between stitches.

a. To hold the garment correctly place canvas side of the garment on table with front edge of garment away from table edge.

b. Fold the lapel edges so that the lapel section is held in the hand with thumb uppermost so as to be free for easing canvas.

On the lapels, start the pad stitch 1 inch behind the break line, paralleling this line from neck edge to edge of garment just below the top button.

a. Locate the break line, and chalk it. This line begins within 1 to 1½ inches below the shoulder seam on the neck edge, depending on the length of the lapel roll, and ends opposite the top button.

b. Chalk a second line 1 inch back of the break line on the garment side.

Using short easy diagonal basting, baste along this line.

c. With even basting stitches, baste from diagonal basting to bottom of garment.

Continue basting rows 2½ inches apart,

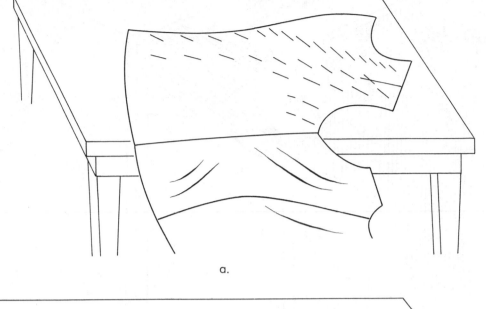

a.

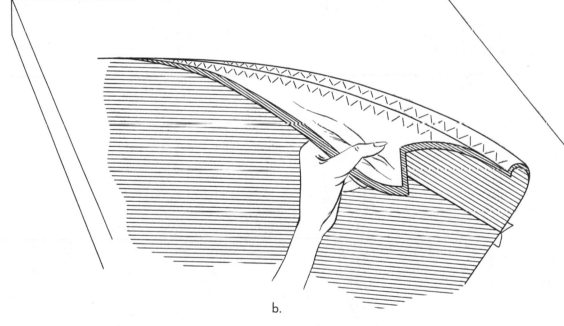

b.

Figure 51

These rows of pad stitches are made to the right and left alternately, sliding the hand from neck to buttonhole to prevent twisting of the canvas. The rows of pad stitches touch on a common line.

Continue the operation to the point of lapel stitching line, slightly easing the canvas with the thumb onto the garment to shape the lapel. Repeat for second side.

TAPING THE GARMENT FRONTS

Figure 52.

a. Lay garment flat on table with canvas up.
  1. Pin tape along back edge of break line, easing break line onto tape ⅛ to ⅜ inch.
     Baste tape into position and hem to canvas along both edges.
     This prevents the break line from

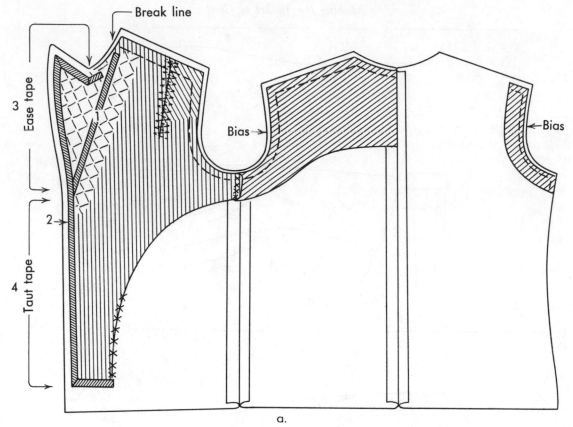

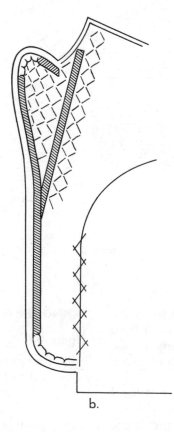

Figure 52

stretching and helps the fit of the garment over the bustline.

2. Trim away the canvas ⅛ inch behind the stitching line along front facing edge from bottom of hem, along the garment edge, around the lapel point to the collar notch.

Later, when you make the garment hem, cut the canvas off across the hem edge.

Tape these stitching edges of the garment fronts with narrow linen, silk, or rayon tape. The tape straddles the canvas edge, the front tape edge being flush with the facing stitching edge.

3. From the top button, around the lapel point, and to the collar notch hold the tape easy. Pin into place and baste.

4. From the top button to the lower garment edge, hold the tape taut.

Place the garment edge along a rule to check whether the tape is too taut or too slack. The garment edge *must* hang perpendicular to floor.

If the lapel or lower garment edges have squared turns, miter the tape.

b. If the lapel or lower garment edges have a curve, the outer tape edge follows the stitching line, and the inner tape edge is notched away to prevent forming of folds.

To insure accurate matching of lapels and curves at lower jacket fronts in both shape and length, carefully check the two sides together after basting on the tape.

Hem the tape lightly to the wool on the outer edge first, then hem the inside edge of tape to the canvas.

The outer tape edge forms the stitching line for the facing.

STEAMING THE TWO FRONTS AFTER TAPING

After the tape is sewed on the fronts, place front lapels over curved pad and steam from the canvas side to the top button, shaping lapels as they are being steamed.

From the top button to bottom of garment is a straight edge, so should be steamed along a ruled line.

Buttonholes may be made in the right hand side of the jacket or they may be left until the facing is sewn on. See "Fastenings on Garments," pp. 77–84.

TAPING UNDERARM OF ARMSCYE

Figure 53.

The matching curved edges of the sleeve and the garment armscye when stitched together have a tendency to stretch and bunch away from the figure at both front and back lower armscye.

To prevent this and to make the armscye hug the figure, you will need to tape the armscye.

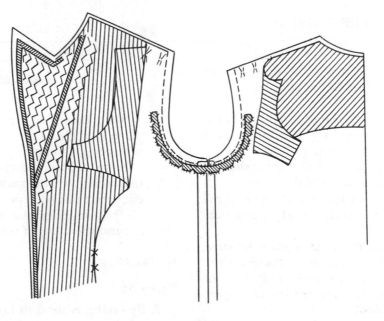

Figure 53

The tape is clipped along one edge to allow it to lie flat when curved around the armscye.

Place an ease thread along the marked stitching line of the under half of the armscye from width of chest to width of back.

Beginning at the width of chest, place the un-clipped edge of tape along ease thread and ease in about ¼ inch of the armscye from chest width to underarm seam and pin into place.

Leave flat across the seam at underarm.

From underarm seam to back width of the armscye, ease from ¼ to ⅜ inch onto the tape and pin into place.

In fabrics that stretch badly it may be necessary to carry the tape up to the back shoulder seam.

Baste the tape first along the armscye stitching line, then along the spread clipped edges.

Hem loosely by hand along both edges.

PULL-UP STITCH

Figure 54.

The pull-up stitch instead of tape may be used around armscye.

Start from the right-hand end, take a stitch ⅛ inch long on the needle, throw the thread from the needle's eye around the needle point from left to right and then pull the needle through the loop. Repeat successive stitches by placing the needle in the hole in the front end of the preceeding stitch. Pull each stitch tightly enough to ease in the amount desired along the stitching line.

ATTACHING FACING TO THE GARMENT

Figure 55.

Place the garment right side up on the table. Match right side of front facing edge to the garment edge.

    a. From top button to top of lapel around to the collar notch, slightly ease facing onto the garment and pin into position.

    b. Across the lapel point ease the facing slightly, or until it forms a blister of the facing.

        This ease allows the seam edges to roll under after being stitched and turned right side out.

    c. From top button of squared garment edge, or from the back of the jacket curve at hem edge, hold the facing slightly taut onto the garment so that the garment hangs perpendicular to the floor.

        Pin edges together and baste.

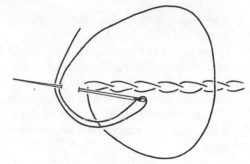

Figure 54

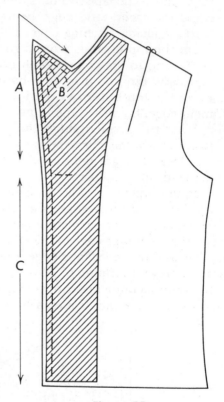

Figure 55

Turn facing to the right side, pin into place, and check for correct fit of the facing onto the garment.

From the taped side of the garment stitch the facing to the garment along the tape edge, but not on tape, from collar notch to the bottom edge of a garment if square, or around the curve if rounded.

FLY FACING

Figure 56.

A fly facing is used to fasten a garment with concealed buttons and buttonholes. The fly is

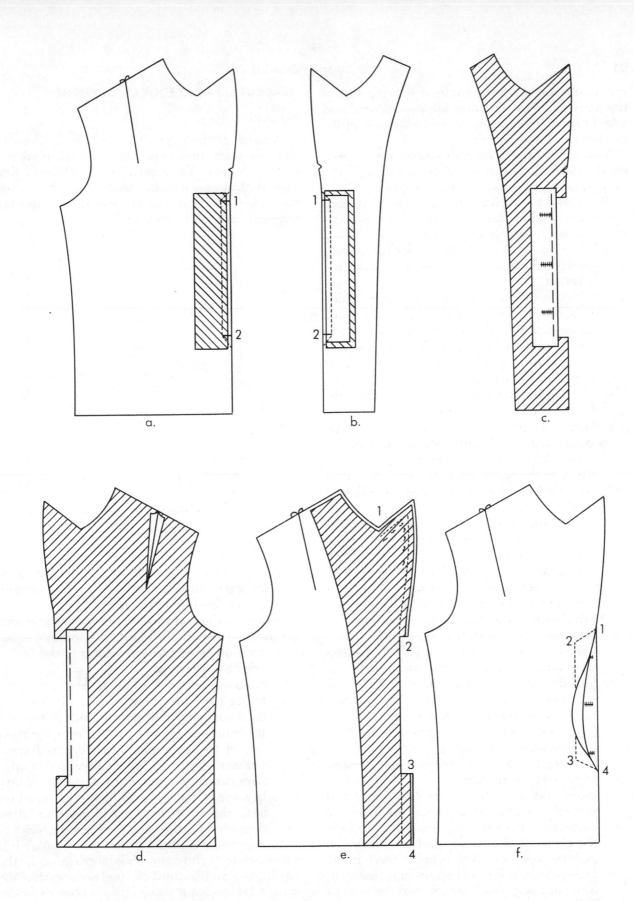

Figure 56

made only on the buttonhole or overlap side of the garment, after the fronts are pad stitched and edges taped. The button or underlap side of the garment is not changed.

The length spaces for buttonholes are marked on the buttonhole side of the front overlap, and on a matching position on its facing.

Two lengths of facings are cut, plus the desired width needed for planned buttonholes, plus ½-inch seams on both sides and ends.

  a. Place one buttonhole facing length on garment with right sides facing and baste into position.

    Stitch in diagonally to tape edge (which forms the stitching edge of garment), stitch along tape to end of facing, then diagonally out to garment edge as indicated by dotted lines. Clip straight in to stitching turn as shown at Points 1 and 2.

  b. The buttonholes are made only through the facing of the garment; therefore, the second facing length *must* be lined with canvas. Baste facing and canvas strips together.

    Stitch diagonally in from edge to seam; stitch along seam edge to end, then turn and stitch out to garment edge as indicated by dotted lines.

    Cut straight in to stitching turn as shown by solid lines at Points 1 and 2.

    Grade seams.

    Steam seam of *a* and *b* wide open.

c, d. Turn facing lengths to wrong sides on garment and facing, roll edges slightly to wrong side, baste, and steam. Remove bastings and resteam to remove basting imprints.

    Rebaste each strip along folded edges until facing is attached and stitched.

  e. Join facing to garment (see Fig. 55, p. 92).

    Stitch from 1 to 2 and from 3 to 4, stitching back on seam ends to prevent ripping.

    Cut off lapel point and grade se .ms.

    Press seams wide open.

    Baste along folded edges, rolling seams slightly to wrong side.

  f. Baste and stitch from 1 to 2 to 3 to 4 and securely fasten thread ends on inside of garment. This stitching is essential to hold the garment, the facing, and the two inside facings together. Buttonholes used in fly facings should be worked by machine if an attachment is available, or may be worked **by hand.**

GRADING SEAMS AT EDGE OF GARMENT

Figure 57.

A seam at the edge of a garment is likely to show the seam imprint and be bulky when pressed right side out. To prevent this bulkiness first trim both seams parallel to stitching line, then trim away ⅛ of that edge of the seam that touches the inner side of the garment.

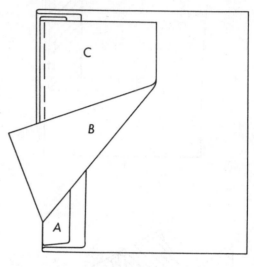

Figure 57

This grading staggers the two seam widths inside the garment edge and produces a smooth appearance from the right side.

Steaming the seam wide open from the wrong side of the garment produces the smoothest seam.

  a. Trim off ⅛ of seam touching *b*, the facing side of the garment.

  c. From the right side of the garment, with the facing edge held toward you, slightly roll the facing edge to the wrong side so that the stitching line does not show from the right side of the garment. This edge is basted, steamed, bastings are removed, and edge is resteamed to remove any basting imprints. In some instances it will be necessary to rebaste this edge when dry in order to follow through on other construction processes.

In a garment with lapels or rolled collar it is necessary to reverse the above operation at the top button and buttonhole positions so that the seam edge does not show either above or below the top button position.

CURVED EDGES

Figure 58.

Inside curve:

a. When an inside curve appears, as an armscye or neckline, the seam is clipped to the stitching line in order to allow the shorter tight edge to spread when pressed away from the stitching line.

Outside curve:

b. Where an outside curve appears, the seam around the curve is notched to the stitching line before the fabric is turned right side out.

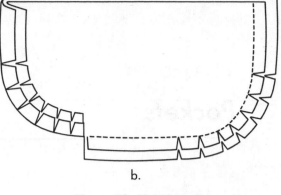

b.

Figure 58 (Continued)

This notched seam prevents folds of seam from appearing within the garment edge.

STITCHING SHOULDER SEAMS

Shoulder seams of the garment have previously been fitted, tailor tacked, and opened up to apply front and back canvas.

Match these tailor tacks exactly in the wool only, pin, baste, stitch, and steam open. Trim seams parallel to stitching lines, leaving ¾-inch seams.

Trim away excess canvas seams, overlap over the wool seam, and sew together by hand, using ¼-inch diagonal basting. Catch stitches through to wool seam to hold canvas securely in place.

Overlap underarm seams of canvas and sew in the same manner.

Machine stitch other seams, neck, and armscye, when the collar and sleeves are attached.

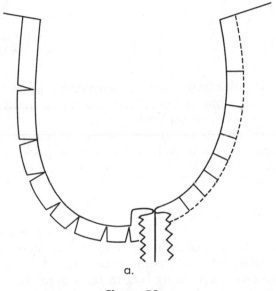

a.

Figure 58

Pockets

Positions for pockets on the garment were tailor tacked after the garment was cut.

Because all persons are not the same size, these positions may need to be changed to keep them in correct proportion to the wearer.

With the garment on the wearer, turn the hem up before the permanent location of the pockets is decided upon. Mark the new pocket location accurately on one side of the garment.

Remove the garment and pin together, accurately matching the two front sections of the garment; and transfer the marked pocket position to the second half of the garment.

If one hip is larger, the garment may be wider on one side of the pocket position. This variance in width should appear from the pocket edge to the side seam of the garment.

All set-in pockets should be reinforced with canvas along the stitching line on the wrong side of the garment. This canvas prevents too great strain on the fabric. The pocket above the bust line already has canvas behind it, but pockets below the waistline will need to be reinforced. In a patch pocket, reinforce the two top corners with canvas on the wrong side of the fabric. Cut the canvas on the same grain as the fabric it is reinforcing.

In patch, welt, flap, or saddlebag pockets match the fabric grain with the garment grain. If a design such as stripes, checks, or plaids appears in the fabric, the design should match the garment in both cross and length grain.

If a decorative idea is desired, cut pockets on the true bias, especially in checks or plaids, or place them on the cross grain.

In a corded or piped pocket use bias because it adjusts more easily to that type of pocket. The bias should always be cut in the same direction from the fabric.

Always cut the grain of the pocket bag the same as the garment grain.

In an inset pocket, one section of the bag is usually of wool and one of lining. To save wool, a narrow strip of wool may be stitched across the upper pocket lining bag instead of making the section entirely of wool.

When a pocket is parallel to the floor, the wool section is always sewed to the upper edge, the lining to the lower edge of a pocket.

In a perpendicular pocket the wool section is sewed to the back edge, the lining to the front edge of the pocket opening.

Check pocket size and length in relationship to the size and scale of the individual.

WELT POCKET

Figure 59.

A welt pocket is made with the welt sewed into the lower edge of an inserted pocket, which may be parallel to the floor, perpendicular to the floor, or on the diagonal.

In whichever direction the pocket is made, the grain and design of the welt, whether of plain,

96

stripes, or plaids, must match the grain and design in the garment when attached. The exception is the welt made on the true bias.

The welt may be made of two thicknesses of wool, as in the flap pocket, or with the outside of wool and the wrong side lined with matching lining silk.

To give crispness to the welt use hymo or its equivalent as interlining, cut the exact size of the finished welt.

a. Cut the three welts, one each of wool, lining, and canvas with the ends cut on the straight grain or on the true bias. This welt when finished is approximately 4 to 5 inches long by 1 or 1¼ inches wide. Allow ½-inch seam on top edge and two ends and ¼-inch seam on edge which is sewed into garment.

b. Place the canvas on the wrong side of the wool, pin into position, and trim away ½-inch seams at one side and the two ends. Baste the canvas into place.

c. Turn the ½-inch wool seams over onto the canvas, miter the corners, and baste into place. Slip stitch the mitered corners, and catstitch the wool to the canvas, making sure the stitches do not appear on the right side of the welt.

d. Fit the lining to the wrong side of the welt, turn under ¼-inch seam, miter corners, and baste along turned seam. Baste the lining into place and slipstitch to the wool seam. Remove all bastings and steam. Place a basting ¼-inch from the raw edge for stitching line.

e. Place the welt into place on the garment, matching the design lines if a design appears in the fabric.

Pin and baste into place at the lower edge of the pocket opening. If stitching is to appear on welt, stitch across top edge only, ending at the turn of stitching at corner; have threads long, pull through to wrong side, and fasten securely.

f. Cut two pocket bag sections, the grain of each of which will match the fabric grain when the finished pocket bag falls into position. Place lower (lining) section over welt with stitching lines matching and baste.

Place upper (wool) section into position with cut edge touching cut edges of welt and bag and baste.

1. Stitch the lower section of bag and welt into position, beginning and ending with machine stitch crowding around the end of the welt, and stitch back 3 or 4 stitches on stitching line to prevent ripping.

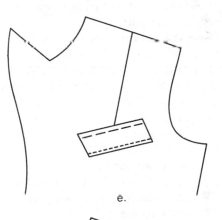

e.

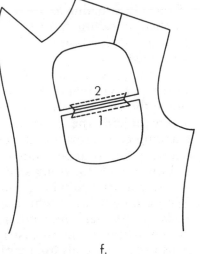

f.

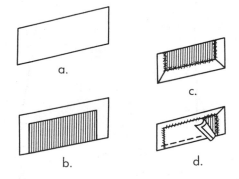

a.

b.

c.

d.

Figure 59

2. Stitch the upper section of bag into position, with stitchings ending 2 or 3 stitches short at each end, to prevent a hole's appearing when pocket is finished. Stitch back on the end of the stitching to prevent ripping.

To check for correct stitching lengths, turn the bag up from the welt ends and check to see that the end stitch hugs the end of the welt closely.

Fold the welt into the correct position into which it will fall when finished; stick pins at welt ends through stitching ends of upper bag. The pins should fall *outside* the stitching ends of the bag stitching line.

Cut the pocket opening between the raw edges of the sections of the bag to within ¼-inch of stitching ends, then diagonally out to the stitching ends. Pull the sections of the bag to the wrong side, which will allow the welt to fall into correct position on the garment.

g. Baste the sections of pocket bag together. With the bag on the machine, fold the garment away at one end of the pocket, adjust the triangle at end of pocket opening into position, and stitch in an arc close against the pocket across the triangle. Continue stitching around the pocket bag and up to the second pocket end where the triangle is to be stitched into position.

h. The welt on the right side of the garment is left standing free. It may be finished in either of two ways.

1. If outside stitching is used, the welt is stitched across the top edge in *e* and the thread ends are fastened securely on the wrong side.

Baste the welt ends to the garment. Stitch the welt ends to the garment. Stitch the welt ends from the lower edge where it joins the garment, up to the stitching end across top of welt, then diagonally out to upper point.

Pull threads to wrong side and fasten securely at each stitching end.

2. Where no outside stitching is used, the ends of the welt may be slip stitched closely to the garment just under welt ends to prevent ends from curling under.

Fasten securely at top welt edges with a few stitches at right angles to pocket ends.

Remove all bastings, steam thoroughly and, if necessary, pound flat with press paddle.

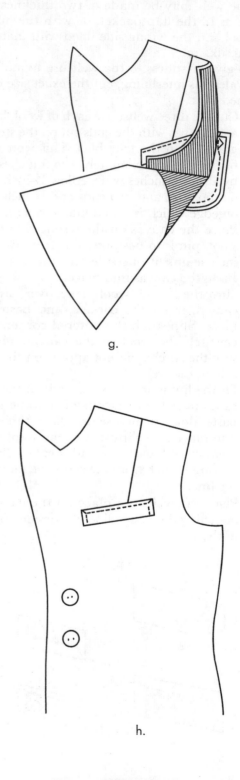

g.

h.

Figure 59 (Continued)

FLAP POCKET

Figure 60.

a. Cut two rectangular pieces of wool approximately 5 inches by 2 inches with ¼-inch seam all around. The flap may be rectangular, curved, or shaped at outer edge.

   Pin the two sections together around outer edge, slightly easing top section onto under section to allow the seam to roll to wrong side, baste, and stitch ¼ inch in from edge. Trim across angles, or notch out curved edges, then press seam wide open.

b. Turn to right side, baste around seam edge, steam, remove bastings, and resteam to remove basting imprints. Make two flaps exactly alike.

   If edge stitching is required on the flap, the stitching should be done before flap is sewed to garment.

c. Baste flap into position with open raw edges touching basted cutting edge of pocket opening.

d. Cut one section of pocket bag of wool and one of lining silk.
   1. Match the stitching line of the wool section to stitching line of flap and baste into position.
   2. Match the stitching line of the lining section to the lower stitching line of pocket opening and baste into position.

Stitch the wool section and flap into place with one row of stitching, being careful that stitching is exact at end of flap. The two stitching ends should be back stitched upon themselves a few stitches to prevent ends from ripping back. Stitch the lower pocket section into place, having the two stitched ends two or three stitches shorter than the upper stitching row. This prevents a hole at the outside ends of the flap when the pocket is finished.

Cut the pocket opening halfway between the two parallel rows of stitching to within ¼ inch from ends. Cut diagonally from center cut to stitching ends of pocket bag. This gives a small triangle at each pocket end. Turn the pocket sections to the wrong side. Fold the triangles at pocket ends back onto the garment.

e. Fold the lower section of bag over the cut seam to form a binding.

   Baste and stitch along binding from the right side of the garment.

   Steam the pocket into position from the right side.

f. From the wrong side, match the two pocket bag sections together and baste.

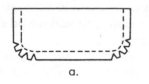

a.

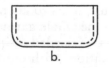

b.

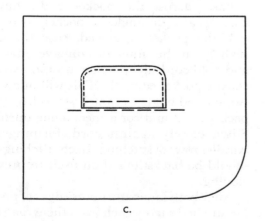

c.

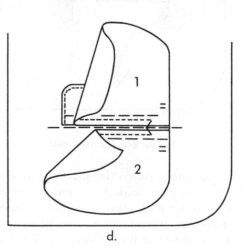

d.

Figure 60

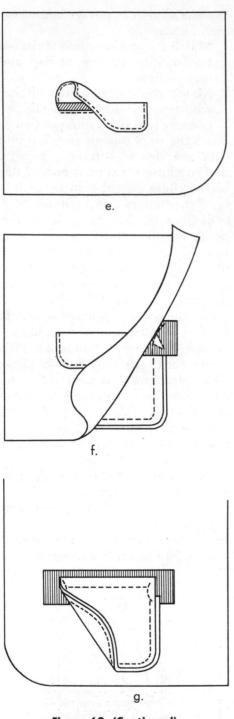

e.

f.

g.

Figure 60 (Continued)

To stitch, place the pocket bag down on the machine, fold the garment away from the pocket end, and stitch two or three times across the triangle in an arc, hugging closely the end of the flap. Continue the stitching around the bag, up and across the triangle at the second pocket end.

g. This shows the wrong side of the pocket bag when completed, with backing canvas behind the stitching line of the flap. On the right side the flap falls down over the pocket opening as indicated in *e*.

CORDED POCKET

Figure 61.

Corded pockets may be made parallel or perpendicular to the floor, on a diagonal, or on a curve.

Usually the material is cut on the true bias, but if the fabric has a stripe and the stripe is used for a trim, the fabric may be cut on the straight grain.

When cutting the bias, always cut the bias in the same direction across the fabric, so that the grain will all run one way.

Cut two strips on the true bias for each pocket, the pocket length plus 1 inch for seams, and 1 inch wide.

a. Fold the bias closely around cord (coarse twine) and sew with fine running stitches as snugly as possible. If matching thread is used, it may be left in when stitched, whereas a contrasting thread would show and need to be removed.

Cut off surplus seam until seam edge from basting is equal in width to corded edge from basting.

b. Locate the pocket positions after the hem is folded up, so as to keep pockets in proportion to the whole garment.

c. Place the two corded strips along marked pocket position, with cut seams touching, pin, and baste into position.

Baste across the pocket ends, having bastings at right angles to pocket opening.

If the pocket is curved, ease the cord slightly on the inner or concave edge (1) and hold cord slightly close on the outer or convex pocket edge (2). This will allow the two corded edges to match smoothly when pocket is cut and cords meet along opening. Stitch closely against cord, forming two parallel rows of stitching. Each stitching end should be backstitched on itself to prevent ripping.

After both inner and outer edges of pocket are stitched survey each from the wrong side to check the accuracy of width between stitchings.

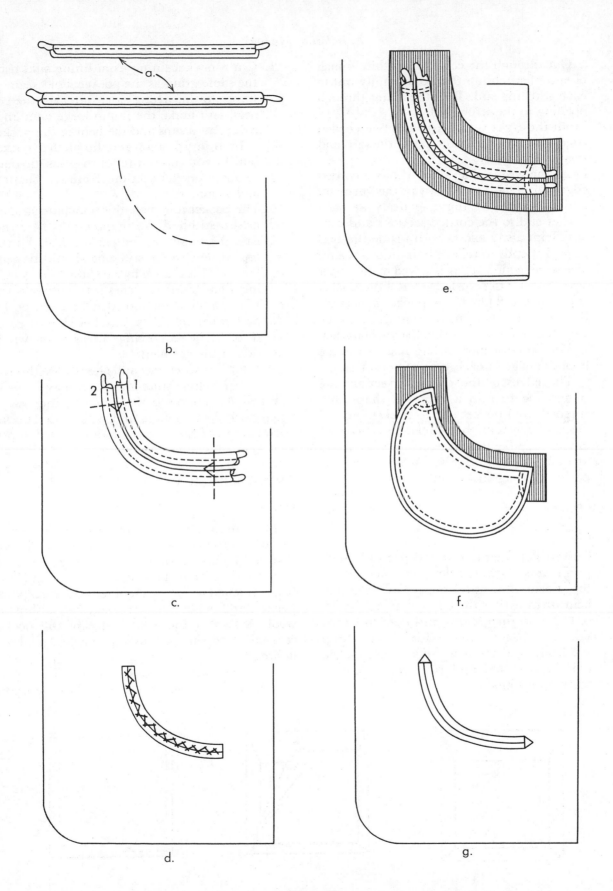

Figure 61

Cut through the center to within ¼ inch of end of stitching, then diagonally out to each stitching end. Turn the seams through opening to the wrong side.

d. From the right side, baste the two corded edges together along the pocket length and steam thoroughly.

e. From the wrong side, stitch the two corded edges on machine, fold away the garment, and stitch the triangle securely at each pocket end to the corded sections and canvas. Trim away excess cord inside the bias at pocket ends to relieve bulk in end seams.

f. The wool section of bag is sewed to the upper seam edge of the corded seam if the pocket is parallel to floor. If the pocket is perpendicular to the floor or on the diagonal the wool bag is sewed to the back seam of pocket.

The lining section of bag is sewed to the opposite edge in each type of pocket used.

The edges of the two bag sections are basted together in a rounded shape and stitched from pocket end to pocket end.

g. Decorative tacks, bar tacks or fabric triangles may be used at each pocket end for attractiveness, and also to reinforce the pocket ends against strain.

PATCH POCKET

Figure 62.

a. Cut pocket the desired width and length, plus seams on three sides and a hem at the top. Baste all around pocket at seam and hem turns. Miter the corners as in Fig. 75, p. 119, and turn seams and hem to wrong side and baste along folded edges. Slip stitch mitered corners. Steam the pocket, remove bastings, and resteam to remove basting imprints.

b. Cut a pocket lining from lining silk, using the same grain as the pocket. Fold seams of lining to the wrong side, mitering the corners, and make the lining large enough to cover raw seams and the hem of the pocket.

Baste into position and slip stitch to pocket, but do not allow stitches to prick through to outer pocket section. Remove bastings and steam.

c. The pocket may be either machine stitched or slip stitched to the garment. In either case the strain on the pocket is at the two top corners where stitching should be reinforced. This is done by carefully hand stitching a few hidden stitches from corner across top just below the top edge, between pocket and garment. These stitches should catch through the reinforcing canvas on the wrong side of the garment.

1, 2. The stitchings indicate two methods of machine stitching which may be used.

When the pocket is slip stitched, the row of stitches should be slightly under the folded pocket edge instead of right on the fold in order to prevent puckering along the edge.

SIMULATED PATCH POCKET

Figure 63.

The simulated patch pocket is one in which the bag sections may be cut entirely of lining, with a 2-inch strip of wool sewed to one section of pocket bag, that showing under the flap. This bag is stitched to the garment to simulate a patch pocket, and is good to use when one is short of wool. A flap at the upper edge of the pocket conceals the opening. This flap may be any shape desired.

a. Cut two wool sections for the flap.

b. Ease the top section of flap onto the under

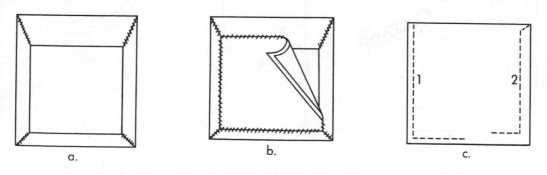

a.   b.   c.

Figure 62

section, so that the seam edges will roll under; pin, baste, and stitch. Clip square across corners or notch curved edges and grade the seams, leaving the wider seam against the right side of flap. Steam seam open, turn to right side, and baste around seam, rolling seam slightly to the wrong side. Steam the flap, remove basting, and resteam to remove basting imprints.

Make a second flap exactly the same size and shape.

c. If you use edge stitching, either machine stitch or pick stitch around the seam the desired width from edge. (Fig. 88, pp. 134, 135.)

d. 1. Mark pocket positions on the garment with bastings parallel to the floor and equidistant from center front.

2. Place right side of flap to right side of garment, flap turned upward, the open edge of flap along the marked pocket, and baste into position. The flap seam should be ¼ inch or less.

e. 1. Cut one bag section the desired length and width from lining silk, plus ½ inch for seams on all edges. This bag must be the same grain as the garment where attached.

2. On the top edge of the bag section, baste a 2-inch strip of wool, and machine stitch along both top and bottom edge.

Closely catstitch across the raw edge of the wool to the lining to prevent raveling.

f. Cut a 2-inch section of matching lining or wool the width of the pocket bag. This section is used to bind the lower edge of the pocket opening opposite the flap edge. This binding section may be of wool if the fabric is light in weight.

g. 1. Place bag section, e, over flap, d, with wool edge facing the flap; baste into place with cut edge matching flap edge.

Machine stitch ¼ inch in from cut edge; stitch bag section and flap into position. To prevent stitching ends from ripping, stitch back several stitches on each end.

2. Place cut edge of binding section at lower edge of basting, touching cut edges of bag section and flap, and baste into position.

Stitch binding section into place, having stitches end two or three shorter than

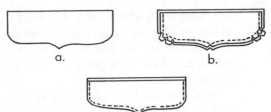

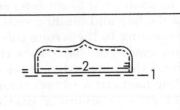

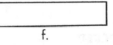

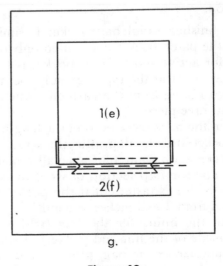

Figure 63

stitching ends above as indicated in dia-gram *g*. This will prevent the open ends of the pocket openings from showing when flap falls into position over pocket opening.

Remove bastings, cut garment between the edges of bag section and facing to within ¼ inch of stitching ends, then diagonally out to stitching ends.

h. Pull the bag and binding sections through the opening to the wrong side of the gar-ment, leaving the flap on the right side.

Bind the lower edge of the opening by folding the narrow section around the seam and baste into position. From the right side, machine stitch along the binding. Catstitch the raw edge to the garment. These stitch-ings will fall under the flap and will not show.

i. Fold the bag down over the bound edge. Place the pocket bag down on the machine, fold the garment away from the open end of the pocket, and stitch the triangle into position in an arc so as to hug the pocket end closely.

j. Baste the bag to the garment. From the right side of the garment stitch the bag into position having the stitching line drop down from flap ends. Bag may be stitched with square or curve at lower turns. The flap may be stitched across the top on the garment edge.

SADDLEBAG POCKET

Figure 64.

The finished saddlebag pocket is similar in size to the patch pocket but is used only on gar-ments for active sports. This pocket is stitched to the garment at the top edge only, permitting the bag to hang from the garment. The pocket is cut in three pieces.

a. Cut the back piece of wool the length of the pocket and the flap, plus the width of the pocket with seam allowance all around.

b. Shape the flap section of wool to suit the individual's taste; cut it the pocket width and from 2 to 3 inches in depth.

c. Cut the lining for the bag (which is the outside of the finished pocket) of wool the same size as the bag, plus ½ inch hem at top. Turn the hem to the wrong side, baste, catstitch, and steam.

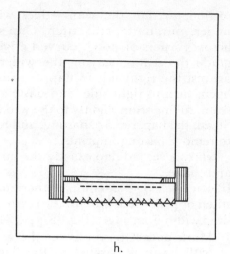

h.

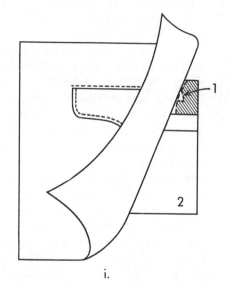

i.

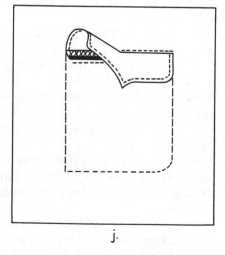

j.

Figure 63 (Continued)

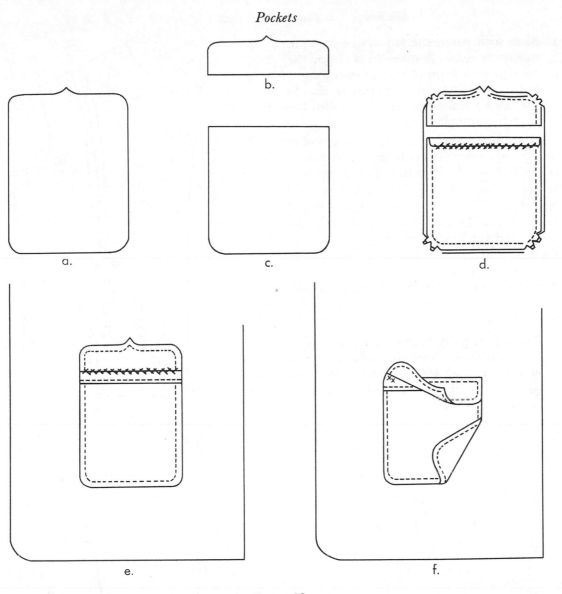

Figure 64

d. Match flap facing (*b*) to the top of the pocket, easing the pocket edge to the facing, pin, baste, and stitch.

Trim away corners to stitching turn, notch out all curves, and grade the seams by trimming the flap (*b*) and the pocket portion (*a*) ⅛ inch narrower than the pocket. Steam seams wide open, turn pocket right side out, baste around all seam edges, slightly rolling the seam to the wrong side.

e. Catstitch the lower raw edge of the flap facing to the pocket. If stitching is used around pocket edge, stitch before the pocket is basted to the garment.

f. Baste the pocket into position on the garment and stitch.

This is done just under the flap along the catstitch at lower flap edge.

Press flap down over pocket opening and stitch across pocket top, matching width from edge to the edge stitching around bag.

POCKET IN A SEAM

Figure 65.

This pocket is made in a construction seam of the garment and may be invisible or have a welt on the outside of the garment.

Cut two shaped pocket bag sections, one of wool and one of lining silk, 8 inches long by 4 inches wide with open edge 4½ inches.

a. 1. Baste and stitch the silk bag section to the front seam slightly back from the construction seam of pocket opening.
2. Baste and stitch the wool bag section to the back seam edge slightly behind the construction edge.

b. Fold wool bag section (2) across seam onto lining bag section (1), baste and stitch. Steam seam (section 2) where bag joins garment.

c. If a welt is used, both pocket bags may be of lining silk. The welt is made and inserted between the silk bag section (*a* 1) and garment, and stitching must follow exactly the garment's stitching edge. (See Fig. 59, p. 97 for making welt.)

From the right side of the garment the welt ends must be sewed securely to the garment

1. by hand slightly under the welt ends.
2. by machine stitching. If stitching is used, stitch the open length edge of the welt first, to turn at ends before being applied to the garment.

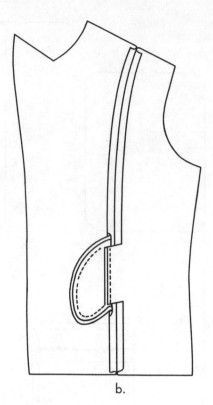

b.

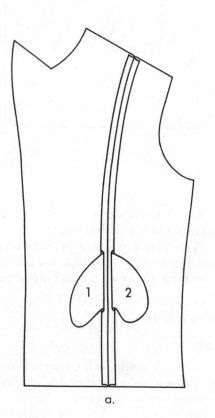

a.

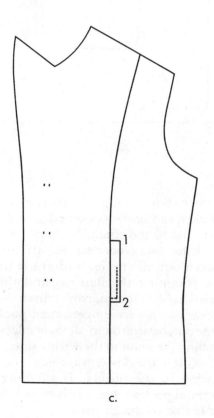

c.

Figure 65

POCKET MADE IN THE DESIGN LINE OF A GARMENT

Figure 66.

When a pocket appears in the design lines of a garment, the pocket will need to be partially made before the garment is basted together. Pocket bag may be cut on side section (*d*) if desired.

 a. Cut pocket section of wool (1) if *c* is used and an additional pocket of lining which will be used for either *c* or *d*.

 b. 1. Baste along the seam edge of the front section of the garment.

  2. Place a cross basting at each finished pocket end on basting line (1).

 c. 1. Baste along the seam edge of the side section of the garment.

  2. Baste pocket bag section of wool into position and stitch ¼ inch below the seam edge so that seam edge does not show when pocket is finished.

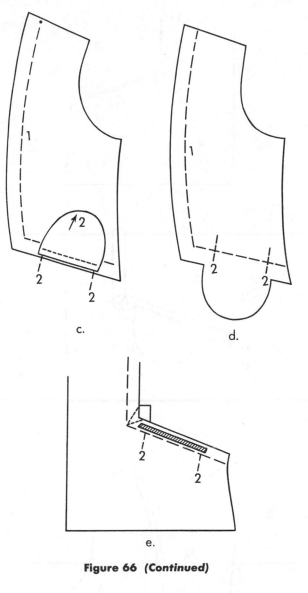

c.

d.

e.

Figure 66 (Continued)

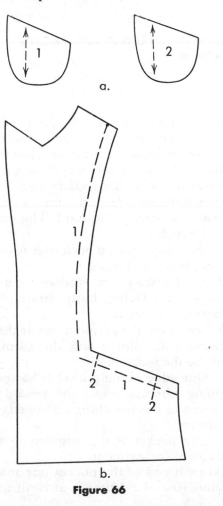

a.

b.

Figure 66

 d. Instead of a separate pocket bag section as in *c*, the bag section may be cut in one with the side section of the garment.

 e. Place a stay tape on the wrong side of the garment, one edge touching the seam edge, with the tape falling out on the seam. Hem both edges of tape lightly to seam.

 f. 1. A reinforced corner is needed at the turn of the seam. (See Fig. 47, p. 85, for instructions in making.)

  2. Baste the silk pocket bag section into position with right sides facing and stitch ¼ inch out on seam from the seam fold. This prevents the bag's showing at folded pocket edge when finished.

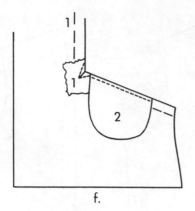

f.

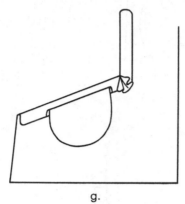

g.

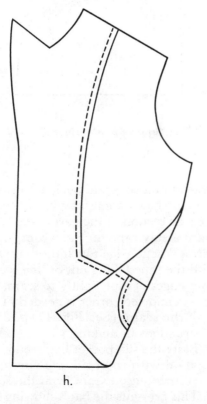

h.

Figure 66 (Continued)

g. Turn the seam edge along basting (as marked in *b* 1), baste, and steam. Remove bastings and resteam to remove basting imprints.

h. Stitch across pocket top the exact pocket opening length, the distance from edge that is planned for the entire seam.

Rebaste seam allowance along *a* from shoulder to turn, then out to underarm seam.

Place Section *a* on Section *c* or *d,* match stitching edges, pin, and baste into place for fitting.

After fitting, stitch the seam from shoulder to front pocket end, leaving long threads to be pulled to wrong side and fastened invisibly.

Stitch the seam from underarm seam to pocket end, with end threads pulled to wrong side and fastened.

Pin two bag sections together, baste, and stitch, beginning and ending stitching at ends of pocket opening.

POCKET BETWEEN LINING AND FACING OF GARMENT

Figure 67.

If there is no pocket on the outside of the garment, one may be inserted at the facing edge between the lining and the garment just above the waistline in the buttonhole side of the garment.

a. Cut two pocket bag sections from lining silk 7 or 8 inches long and 4 inches wide, with seams allowed all around. The open edge is 4½ inches.

Turn each straight open edge to the wrong side, baste, and steam.

b. Baste the two pocket sections together with right sides facing, baste around the bag curve, and stitch.

c. When lining the garment, insert the pocket between the lining and the garment just above the waistline.

One edge of the pocket is basted to the lining stitching edge; the second edge is basted to the matching facing edge of the garment.

The pocket is slip stitched to the two edges of the garment.

d. At each end of the pocket one may use a short row of catstitches at right angles to

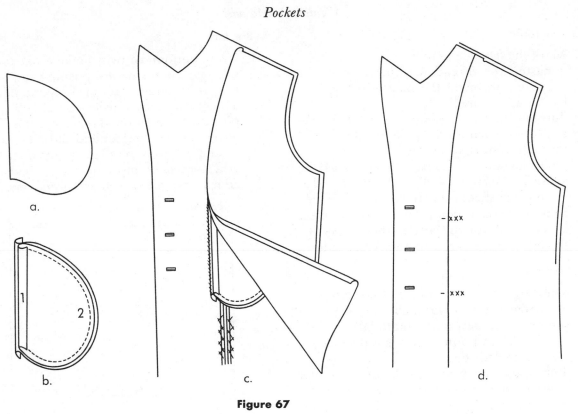

Figure 67

the facing edge to hold the pocket ends securely into position.

DECORATIVE TACKS

Figure 68.

Decorative tacks are used to finish the ends of piped or corded pockets, at stitching ends of pleats, or at dart ends. The base of the decorative tack touches the end where used.

a. Arrowhead:

1. Mark the arrowhead by basting a triangle at the desired position. The two sides of the triangle may be curved inward as in 2 to form a more slender tack.

   Using matching buttonhole twist, start the arrowhead by fastening the thread within the tack and bring the needle out at the left-hand angle at base.

   Take a stitch across the angle opposite the base, placing the needle from right to left parallel to base.

2. On the base line push the needle through at the angle at right and bring out the needle point on base line within the first stitch at the left angle.

3. Repeat the cycle until the stitches on base line touch at center, and the stitches across point opposite base widen out from angle point, ending halfway down sides.
4. Push needle to wrong side and fasten to prevent ripping.

   Stitches should touch each other closely without fabric underneath showing through.

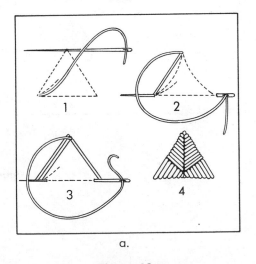

a.

Figure 68

b. Crow's foot:

1. Mark the triangle as in *a.*
   Fasten the thread within center of the triangle and bring the needle through at left angle on base.
2. Turning the triangle from right to left, take a stitch at each angle, pushing the needle through from right to left.
3. Each successive stitch widens across the angle as the stitches fill in down the sides. Each stitch should touch closely.
4. Repeat the operation until the stitches meet on each side of the angle; then carry the thread through and fasten to wrong side.

c. Fabric tack:

1. Cut a triangle the desired finished size plus a narrow seam along each side, with the *base* on the *straight* of the material.
   Miter each point and baste down with knot on folded edge.
2. Turn seams down along sides of the angles to wrong side, baste, and steam.
3. Place the *base* of the triangle into position on the garment, baste into place, and slip stitch closely to garment just under the folded edge.

d. Bar tack:

1. Using buttonhole twist make a bar tack by taking several stitches, pushing the needle in and bringing it out of the same holes.
2. The bar may be finished by closely wrapping the thread around these several stitches, or by buttonholing around the stitches.
   The bar may be placed within the end of a corded or piped pocket, which gives added strength as well as attractiveness.

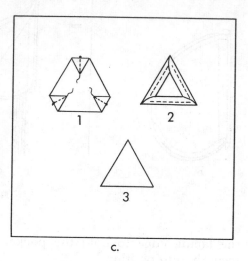

c.

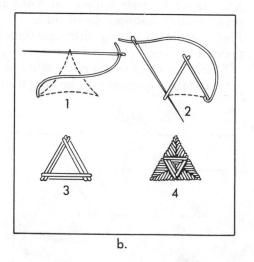

b.

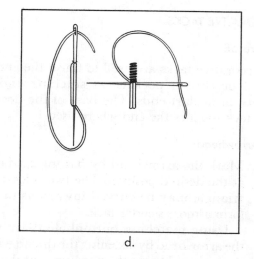

d.

Figure 68 (Continued)

Collar

MAKING THE COLLAR

Figure 69.

The upper section of the collar has been cut with center back on the length grain, and a basting down center back.

The under sections of both collar and canvas have been cut with center back on the bias, with a seam in each.

a. Stitch seam at center back of wool undersection and steam open.

b. Overlap seam edges of canvas and stitch with two parallel stitchings. Trim off excess.

c. Indicates upper wool collar with center back basting.

d. Place under wool collar on table, wrong side up. Place canvas collar on wool, center backs matching, and loosely baste the two together along the neck edge only.

e. Pin neck edge seam of collar to garment. Adjust on dress form or on self, and pin fronts together along button section.

Mark one half side of collar fold from center back toward front where fold touches front break line, 1 and 2.

f. Remove collar from garment and mark second side from marked side, chalking along marked edge.

This break fold to neck edge forms the collar stand.

Pad stitch collar stand.

Hold canvas side of collar neck edge toward you and start pad stitching at one side of center back, pad stitching across in an arc parallel to marked stand to other side of center back.

Repeat several rows of pad stitching, alternating direction to keep canvas from slipping to one side on wool.

Point each stitch taken toward center back at neck edge.

Pad stitch to within ½ inch of stand mark, shaping collar back to an inside curve to fit back neck.

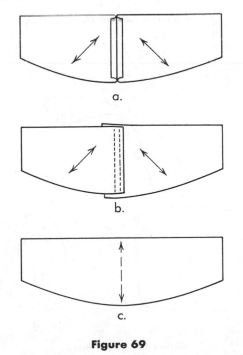

Figure 69

111

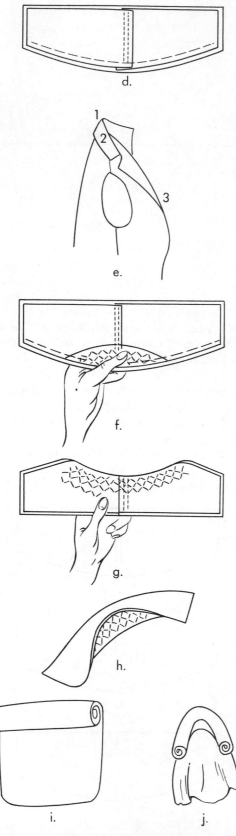

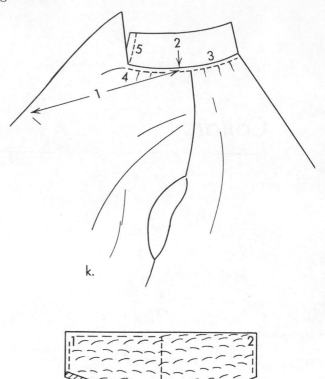

Figure 69 (Continued)

Figure 69 (Continued)

g. Reverse collar with outside collar edge held in hand, with collar over forefinger between thumb and middle finger. This allows easing canvas over the under collar with the thumb as one pad stitches. Ease more canvas over break line fold because of the sharp turn at this point.

Continue pad stitching alternately across collar and ease canvas in as needed to shape collar into correct position as it should appear on the neck of wearer.

h. Collar showing shape when pad stitched.

i. Roll a Turkish towel from end to middle until it forms a roll 2 or more inches thick. Shape into curve until inner curve is neck size.

j. Fit pad stitched collar over curved towel and steam into correct shape with steam iron or with damp cloth over collar. Collar may be pinned to dress form to dry thoroughly or left on curved towel.

k. Mark collar length.

1. Break line of lapel which meets the collar stand at neck edge.
2. End of collar stand.

   Pin and baste collar to neckline of garment.
3. Pull up ease thread around neck of garment and ease neck edge onto collar to where collar stand meets the break line of garment front.

   One inch across point 2, ease the collar onto the neck edge of garment.
4. Lapel notch. Continue pinning to this notch, easing neck to the collar.
5. Mark collar end where it touches notch of lapel at front. Remove collar from garment and mark second half of collar from the first. Place a basting or pencil line across each newly marked collar end.

   Attach upper and under collar.

   Place under collar on table with right side up.

   Place upper collar to under collar with right sides together and center backs matching.

   Pin center backs of collars together.

   Holding collar in hand, begin at center back and slightly ease upper collar to under collar, along outer stitching edge and across ends. Repeat for second side, easing same amount along edge and end. Baste and stitch.

   If collar has square turn, cut off point.

   If collar has rounded edges, notch out surplus curve at seam edge. Grade seams and press wide open.

   Turn collar right side out and baste along folded edge, rolling seam slightly to under side.

l. Finishing collar.

1. Using easy diagonal stitches, begin at Point 1, baste to end 2, then return to 1. Repeat until upper collar is entirely basted to under collar. Shape the upper collar to fit smoothly over the under collar when basting.
3. When collar is finally shaped, trim the neck edges of upper and under collar until the two edge seams are flush.

   Steam into shape, remove bastings, re-steam to remove any basting imprints, and place on form or shaped towel to dry.

Rebaste loosely with diagonal stitches until collar is basted into garment.

Place a basting thread all around stitching line of both under and upper collar neck edge. These two bastings *must* fall one on top of the other.

JOIN COLLAR TO GARMENT

Figure 70.

a. The neck of garment already has an ease thread at stitching line.

   Match facing and garment neck edges; transfer neck seam position to facings and put in ease thread.

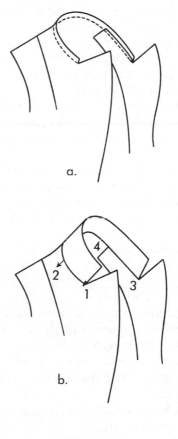

Figure 70

b. Match collar ends tightly into lapel notch and pin stitching seams together.

   Match center backs of collar and garment, and pin.

   Pin collar to garment, matching stitching lines. Beginning at collar end, ease neck to collar up to within ½ inch of garment break line, 2.

Across collar stand, ½ inch on either side of 2, ease collar to neck edge, continue basting collar to center back, easing neck onto collar. Repeat for second collar side. On under side of collar, ⅛ inch behind collar notch 1, tack collar and neck edges together with several tiny stitches, using matching sewing silk. This holds the collar end tightly into lapel notch while stitching. The facing may be joined to collar by machine stitching or by slip stitching.

To machine stitch, baste upper collar and facings together, easing facing to collar.

Check collar on figure before stitching. The collar should hug the neck closely. The seam around the back neck of collar *must not show*. Stitch collar.

Beginning at under collar end, start machine stitching at end of lapel stitching and continue to end of lapel stitching at second collar end. Fasten thread ends securely.

Beginning at upper collar end, start machine stitching at end of lapel stitching and stitch upper collar and facing together. Fasten thread ends securely.

If collar is correctly stitched, the notch will form a sharp **V**, and the stitching seams appear to be continuous from lapel through collar.

Clip seams almost to stitching along collar neck edge.

Steam all neck seams wide open.

Cut away any bulk at inside collar seams to form smooth outside appearance. Hymo may be trimmed to stitching line.

Match stitching seams of collar and facing from notch to shoulder, curve slightly outward toward shoulder and pin together.

Clip back neck seam of outer collar between shoulder seams. Match the two back collar seams, pin and baste.

Sew neck collar seam securely to garment seam, using combination stitch.

    3-4. If the material is firm, the facing and upper collar edges may be slip stitched from notch to shoulder. Turn seams of both collar and lapel to wrong side and baste along fold. Baste by whipping the two folded edges together, slightly easing facing onto collar. Slip stitch the two edges very closely. The collar is then finished as in directions above.

SHAWL COLLAR

Figure 71.

A garment with shawl collar is one in which the under collar and front are cut in one piece. It has a seam at center back in both upper and under collar.

The garment with shawl collar is handled differently from the garment with a separate collar.

Make reinforced corners at seam turn of collar and shoulder seam.

Baste, fit, stitch, and steam all shoulder seams and collar.

Hymo is cut exactly like the garment front with seams or darts fitted to match the garment.

Hymo is fitted, pinned into place, and basted onto the two garment fronts and collar.

   a. Canvas collar seams are overlapped at center back and may be basted together with diagonal bastings or stitched by machine.

   b. Neck edge of hymo is basted across back neck of garment and along shoulder seam and stitched by machine or fastened by hand to the neck and shoulder seams of the garment.

   c. Place garment on figure and fasten down center front. The fold formed along collar edge from buttonhole around neck to button is the front break line and the back collar stand. Chalk this line from center back to center front on one side only.

      Remove garment, and chalk second side from first marked stand.

   d. Baste hymo to wool garment 1 inch on the garment side from the chalked stand line, using diagonal bastings.

   e. Baste hymo (below basted line along stand) to the garment, with basting rows 2 inches apart and parallel to center front of garment.

   f. Leave free collar and hymo from *stand* line to collar edge.

   g. Sew the shoulder seams of hymo and garment together securely by hand, using diagonal stitches.

   h. Baste the armscye edges of hymo and garment together 1½ inches from armscye.

   i. Chalk an arc on the hymo from shoulder seam to shoulder seam, curving the arc ½ inch below the collar stand at center back.

      Pad stitch this arc in exactly the same way as in a separate collar. (Fig. 69*f*, p. 112.)

   j. From shoulder and collar turn at neck edge,

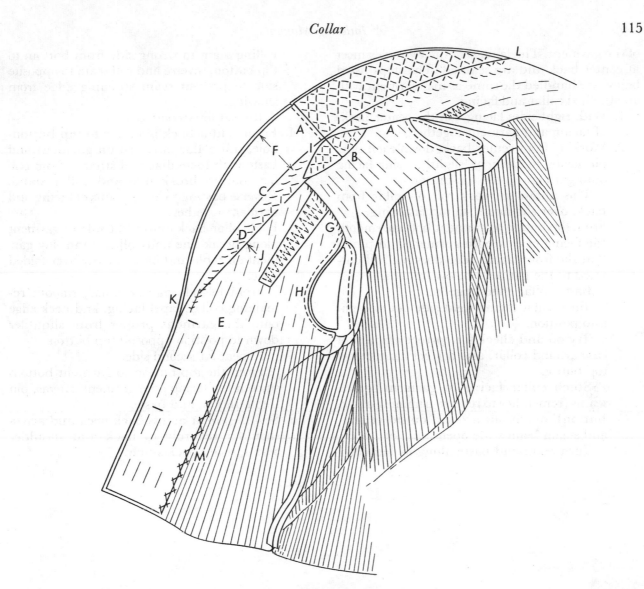

Figure 71

draw a line to top button. Pad stitch the space between this line and diagonal stitch *d*.

k, l. Beginning at 1, the top button on basting line *d*, pad stitch a continuous line the entire length of the collar to the top buttonhole, *k*. Continue pad stitching the entire collar, alternating each row, to prevent the canvas from twisting on the garment. When pad stitching, hold the loose open edges of the collar and hymo in the hand with the garment against the fingers so that the thumb is free to ease the hymo onto the collar to shape while pad stitching.

m Loosely catstitch the back edge of the hymo below curved edge to bottom of garment, making stitches at least 1 inch apart.

TAPING THE SHAWL COLLAR

The garment with shawl collar is taped from the bottom of the garment to the top button, pinning the tape slightly taut along the garment stitching edge to keep the garment edge hanging perpendicular to the floor.

Sometimes the tape may be carried upward on the collar edge toward the shoulder if fabric has a tendency to stretch.

Tape should not be carried around shoulders and back edge of collar as it causes too tight an edge on the collar.

FACING THE SHAWL COLLAR

The facing for the shawl collar, which is the upper collar, is cut in one with the front facing of the garment. The facings of the two sides meet at center back and are seamed. The steps listed below are handled the same as in a garment with an attached collar and facing.

1. With right sides facing, pin the center backs of facing and garment together.
2. Working from center back, down each side, pin facing to garment, slightly easing facing onto garment to the top button.

   This allows an easy roll of collar from back, over shoulders, to top fastening.
3. From top button to garment bottom, smooth the facing closely onto garment and pin so that the front facing edge does not roll outward to the garment below buttons.

   Baste collar edges together.

   Turn collar facing right side out and pin into position.

   Try on and check for correct amount of ease around collar, also correct hang below top button.

   Stitch collar facing to garment, grade seams (remember to reverse trimming at top button), notch out around outside curve, and steam seam wide open.

   Turn seam and baste along folded edge, rolling seam to wrong side from bottom to top button, reverse and roll seam to opposite side to prevent seam stitching edge from showing.

   Repeat for second side.
4. From center back of collar to top buttonhole, roll collar outward on garment and baste with loose diagonal stitches from collar edge to break line and collar stand. Reverse basting to keep grains of facing and garment together.
5. Fold collar back onto right side of garment along break line and collar stand, lay garment on table and baste loosely over folded edge.

   From folded edge of collar, smooth remaining collar, lapel facing, and neck edge onto the garment proper from shoulder down to position opposite top button.

   Repeat for second side.

   From the top button to garment bottom smooth the facing onto garment canvas, pin into position, and baste.
6. Sew the collar across back neck and across shoulder securely to neck and shoulder seams, using back stitch.

Collarless Garments

Figure 72.

In all garments without collars an ease thread or stay stitching should be placed around the neck to prevent stretching while fitting or handling. In a cardigan the stay should extend down the front through the bias section to where the grain straightens out.

a, b. In a cardigan that fits flat against the body or in a jacket that buttons up to the neck with or without a collar, the canvas will not need to be pad stitched; however, all edges will need to be taped to prevent stretching.

c, d. In a cardigan that is built up around the neck, the front curve below the neck will need pad stitching, so that the garment will roll away from the body.

e, f. In a garment with a high round neck which rolls away from the body at the neck edge, or one that is worn either buttoned or left standing open, the neck will need pad stitching so that it will look equally well whichever way it is worn.

In *c, d* and *e, f,* ease the tape slightly along the section which rolls away from the body. Also ease the facing slightly from shoulder to lower edge of roll, then hold taut below the rolled section.

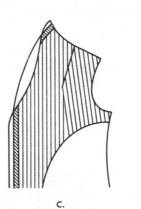

c.

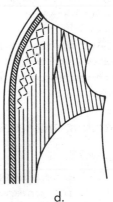

d.

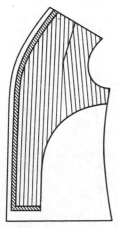

a.

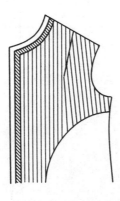

b.

e.

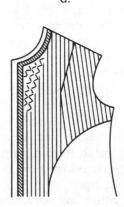

f.

Figure 72

117

Sleeves

FITTING SLEEVES INTO THE WOOL GARMENT

After the collar has been basted on the garment the sleeves are fitted into the armscye (see Fig. 23 on pp. 50–53).

The armscye and matching sleeve seams were carefully cross-marked in the muslin garment. These marks were transferred to wool armscye seams when cut.

Match these marked seams, pin and baste the sleeves into the garment, and try on for checking since the wool may handle differently. Make any necessary alterations.

STITCHING THE SLEEVES

Figure 73.

The sleeve is not stitched until it has been fitted into the armscye to make sure of the correct fit and dart locations.

The diagram indicates the direction in which seams and darts are stitched.

Without removing the sleeve from the armscye, stitch darts at elbow and sleeve cap if used.

Darts at elbow are steamed on wrong side with folded dart edge turned toward the cap.

Darts at sleeve cap are split open and steamed with seams wide open.

Stitch length seam, trim parallel to stitching line, leaving seam ½ or ¾ inch wide, and steam wide open.

Stitch armscye, trim seams parallel to stitching line, leaving ½-inch seam; clip seams almost to stitching line and steam seams wide open if the sleeve is plain. If the upper section of the sleeve

seam seems too bulky, notch out until seam lies flat against garment.

If the sleeve has darts at shoulder, steam the upper half of sleeve seam toward the garment side of the armscye, and the under half of the seam wide open.

If a padded effect is desired around upper half of sleeve cap, press the seams into the sleeve side of the garment.

A narrow bias strip of wigan or felt may be sewed across the upper half of the sleeve cap and

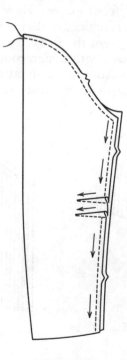

Figure 73

pressed into the armscye, filling out the cap ease and giving a smooth cap fit to the upper arm.

On the under section of the sleeve seam (that part which has been taped and pressed wide open) press the sleeve and garment tightly together to give a sharp turn under the arm.

Should it be necessary to remove the fitted sleeve from the armscye for stitching any portion of the sleeve, you *must* tailor tack the sleeve and armscye all the way around with tacks ½ inch apart. After stitchings are complete, refit the sleeve to armscye, carefully matching each tailor tack. After basting, check the sleeve for correct fit before stitching.

MARKING HEMS OF THE SLEEVES AND JACKET

Figure 74.

To hang the hems of the lining of the sleeves and lower edge of the suit or coat, place the garment right side out on the figure or on a dress form and adjust the lining so that all length seams match those of the garment.

1. Place pins parallel to the floor 6 inches above the lower fold of the sleeve edge, pinning the lining and the garment sleeves together.
2. Place pins parallel to the floor 3 to 6 inches above the jacket or coat hem edge, pinning the lining and the garment together, leaving enough space below pins to work with the lining hem.

Figure 74

MITERED CORNER

Figure 75.

A mitered corner should be used on squared turns along the cut edge of fabric to prevent frayed edges from appearing, also to eliminate bulk where a hem or seam appears along two converging edges.

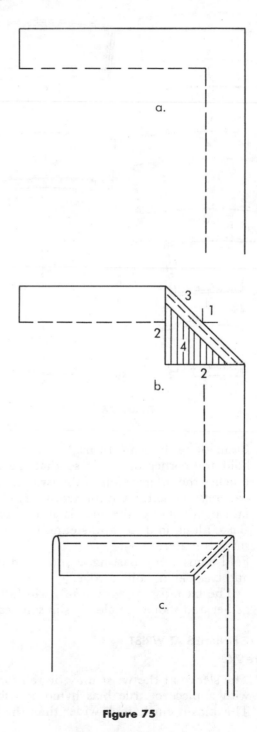

Figure 75

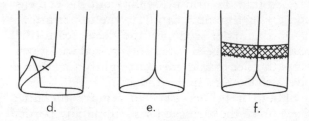

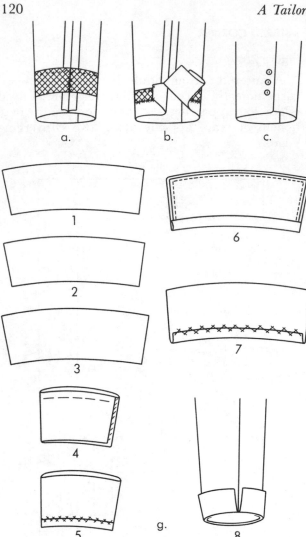

Figure 76

a. Baste along the seam turns.

b. Fold the corner of fabric so that the fold touches the intersection of the two merging bastings (1), and have the grains (2) of the fabric fall along the grains underneath. Baste along fold (3) and steam. Cut away surplus material (4).

c. Fold hems along basting as indicated in *a*, and baste along folded edge.

   The basted bias edges (*b*-3) will fall together and should be closely slip stitched.

SLEEVE FINISHES AT WRIST
Figure 76.

a. The sleeve at the wrist may be reinforced with a piece of true bias hymo or wigan. This bias is cut ½ inch wider than the fin-

ished hem and slightly longer than the circumference of finished wrist edge.

With the sleeve wrong side out, stretch the bias slightly and pin and baste into place with the lower edge of the canvas touching the fold of the sleeve hem. Overlap bias ends at sleeve seam and sew together. Sew the top edge of the canvas to the sleeve, using French hem.

Turn the hem of garment up over bias, pin, baste, and catstitch hem edge to the canvas.

b. If the sleeve is two-piece and has a vent or placket at the back or elbow seam, the upper part of the sleeve overlaps the under seam so that one looks across instead of into the opening when the forearm is held parallel to floor. From the wrong side the lower edge of the canvas is placed along the sleeve fold and at the overlapping end; the bias end is in line with the sleeve seam.

Pin, baste into place, and French hem along upper edge of bias.

1. The overlap edge of vent and the hem turn-up should be mitered to insure a smooth finish at opening (see Fig. 75, p. 119).

   The top of the hem is catstitched to the bias.

   From the right side match the two vent or placket edges and baste.

   From the wrong side of the sleeve, pin the underlap into place, baste, and catstitch closely the width of the hem.

c. When a vent or placket is used, two or three buttons may be used as decorations.

d. If buttons are not used, a short French tack may be used to hold the vent edges together.

e, f. The sleeve may have a shaped opening at the wrist. This sleeve will need to be finished with a fitted or shaped facing. *f* shows the wrong side with canvas under the hem. This sleeve may also be turned up at the bottom to form a narrow self cuff.

g. Cuffs are frequently used on sleeves. A cuff which is an extension of the sleeve proper is much simpler to make than a separate cuff which must be attached. When a separate cuff is used, the sleeve is finished as in *a*, with the hem turned back and catstitched to the canvas. If the fabric is firm, the canvas may be eliminated in the sleeve and used only in the cuff. The cuff is completely finished before it is attached to the sleeve, eliminating a bulky seam edge at the wrist.

The cuff should be made slightly larger than the sleeve since the sleeve edge is a smaller circle fitting inside the larger cuff circle.

Cuffs may be open at the ends, or they may be sewed into a circle. In either case the cuffs are finished before they are sewn to the sleeve.

1. Cut two inner sections of fabric the cuff size plus ⅜-inch seams at ends and across top.
2. Cut two hymos the same size as 1.
3. Cut two outer sections of fabric with ⅜-inch seams at ends and across top, and ½-inch seam at lower edge.
4. Cuff in a circle. Fit the inner section of fabric around the wrist of the garment for correct size.

    Pin, baste, stitch, and steam seam.

    Fit the hymo onto the wrong side of the cuff, slightly easing hymo onto cuff. Overlap seams and sew together with short diagonal bastings.

    Ease the outer section of fabric over the hymo, baste, stitch, and steam seam.

    Stitch the three sections together around the top edge, grade the seam, press open, and turn cuff right side out.

    Roll the seam edge to the wrong side, baste, steam, remove basting, and resteam to remove basting imprints.

5. Turn the wrist edge seam of outer cuff section around the raw edge and baste up on the under cuff section. Catstitch over raw edge, but do not allow stitches to prick through to outer cuff section. Repeat for second cuff.
6. Cuff open at ends. Measure the inner fabric section around sleeve wrist for correct size and mark each cuff end for stitching line.

    Slightly ease canvas onto the fabric across the top edge and baste. Slightly ease the outer fabric section over the hymo, pin, baste, and stitch the three sections together across each end and along top edge.

    Grade seams, notch out curved turns or trim across angles, steam seam open, and turn cuff right side out. Baste around cuff, slightly rolling seam edge to the wrong side.

7. Turn the ½-inch seam around lower cut edge to the wrong side, baste, and catstitch over raw edges.

    Steam cuff, remove bastings, and resteam.

    From the wrong side slip stitch the two cuff edges together ½ inch, the width of the turned up seam.

8. Fit the wrist edges of cuff and sleeve together and closely slip stitch just above the cuff edge. This method of making and joining cuffs to the sleeve leaves less bulk at wrist than the method of joining cuff to the sleeve with a facing.

BIAS FOR BINDING
Figure 77.

Cutting and joining bias:

a. *Cutting Bias.* To cut a true bias a piece of fabric is folded so that the warp or length grain falls along the woof or cross grain. The bias formed is a true bias. Cut bias the desired width.

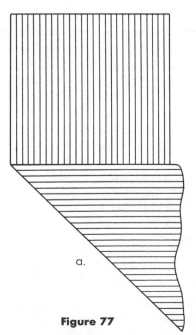

Figure 77

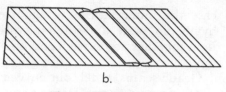

Figure 77 (Continued)

Fabric should always be folded from the same angle on the fabric, otherwise the design in the fabric will not match.

All bias used as a trim or a binding should be cut on the true bias.

b. Joining Bias. All ends of bias should be cut along the length grain of the fabric so that when bias is joined the length grain runs in the same direction throughout the bias strip.

BOUND EDGE

Binding used on the edges of a garment is usually cut on the true bias of the material. For a decorative effect the binding may be cut on the cross or length grain if a stripe is used.

Bias must all be cut in one direction; otherwise, when joining the bias in a seam or in making buttonholes or pockets, the design in the twill, stripe, or plaid will not match. It is recommended that a trial sample be made on a scrap of material to see which gives the best effect before applying to the garment.

Bias is cut twice the width of the finished edge plus two seams.

Place the bias to the garment edge with right sides facing and stitching edges matching. Stretch the bias slightly onto the garment edge to prevent fullness on the bias edge. Pin and baste into position and miter any angle turns.

On an outside curved edge ease the bias slightly along the stitching edge to allow folded edge of the bias to lie flat when finished. On an inside curve stretch the bias slightly to prevent the fold edge of the bias from rippling.

Machine stitch from garment side along marked stitching edge.

Steam the bias away from the stitching line toward the cut edge.

Measure from the stitching on the bias the exact width desired; fold the bias to the wrong side and baste along folded edge.

From the wrong side of the garment, fold under the bias edge, leaving the bias just wide enough to cover the machine stitching, and baste into place.

Closely slip stitch the bias into position, concealing the machine stitches. Remove all bastings and steam.

FITTED OR SHAPED FACING

A fitted or shaped facing is one which is cut exactly like the edge of the garment to be faced, but the inside may parallel the contour edge or may be cut any shape one desires.

The facing may be used on the wrong side when a collar or a cuff is not used on a garment, or where the edge of a garment is not hemmed back on itself. The facing also may be used as a decorative finish on the outside of the garment, as self facing, a contrasting facing. If the fabric has a design such as stripes or checks, it may be used on the bias or on the reverse stripe.

To cut the pattern, use either the original pattern or the garment edge to be faced; place the pattern edge on a new piece of pattern tissue and trace around the stitching edge and seams.

Remove the pattern from the tissue, plan and mark the inside edge of the facing with pencil to the exact width and shape desired.

Seams *must* be added on all edges of the facing pattern, before it is cut out. Cut the fabric from the new pattern on the same grain as edge to be faced, and mark all stitching lines with chalk or basting lines.

When facing the *inside* of a garment, ease the garment slightly onto the facing. When using the facing on the *outside* of the garment, ease slightly onto the garment.

Stitch all seams in the facing and steam open before applying to the garment, and match all seams.

FASTENING SHOULDER PADS TO GARMENT

After the sleeves are stitched at armscye, put the garment on dress form or figure and permanently adjust both shoulder pads into position under the front facing. Usually the outer edge of pad extends approximately ½ inch beyond armscye stitching edge, depending on fashion and appearance. Pin securely into position from right side of garment so that when the pad is sewed to garment there will be no slippage.

Pads are sewed to canvas from armscye toward neck where point of pad is securely anchored to shoulder seam. Where the pad falls along armscye seam, sew the two together with a loose stab stitch and securely anchor each pad end to armscye seam, using a double strand of mercerized cotton.

In a raglan or kimono sleeve use the curved shoulder pad and adjust it until it gives the best shoulder shape from right side of garment. Sew the pad securely to the shoulder seam or seams.

Hemming the Jacket or Coat

HEMMING THE JACKET

Figure 78.

Lead weights:

Lead weights are used in jackets, if necessary, at underarm and back seams to hold the jacket in place on the figure.

  a. The weights are slipped into cases or pockets made from the lining silk of the garment.

  b. The pockets are sewed securely to the hem edge of the jacket before hem is sewed to the garment.

Jackets that are to be lined will have the hems French hemmed or catstitched at lower edges of sleeves and garment.

If the jacket is unlined, the hem will be bound as in Fig. 35, pp. 70, 71.

Figure 79.

  a. 1. On the jacket, the hem is finished to the back edge of the front facing.
  2. Shows taped edge of garment.
  3. Shows hymo of garment.
  4. Baste the hem edge through the facing and the section of the jacket covered by the facing.

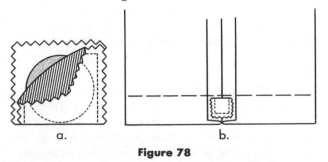

  a.   b.

Figure 78

5. ⅜-inch seam is allowed below 2.
6. Surplus material is cut away.

  b. Turn the ⅜-inch hem in *a* to the wrong side and baste along the fold. Fit the facing back onto garment and baste into place.
  1. Catstitch facing loosely to canvas, using ½ to 1 inch between stitches.
  2. Catstitch over raw edge of facing to hem edge, using ¹⁄₁₆- to ⅛-inch stitch lengths.
  3. Slip stitch open edge of facing closely to garment.

If the lower edge of the jacket is rounded, tape the rounded edge to the back edge of the canvas. Stitch the facing and garment together around the curve to the end of the tape. Finish the hem as in the jacket above.

  c. 1. In the jacket, turn up the surplus lining hem to the wrong side so that the folded edge is ¾ inch above the jacket hem. Mark the hem of the lining the same width of the jacket hem, and trim off the surplus.
  2. Baste the lining to the garment ½ inch above the folded edge of the lining. Leave the 1½-inch center back ease basted in place so that the lining and garment between underarm seams are the same size.
  3. Fold the loose edge of the hem below 2 back onto the garment along the basting line. Slip stitch the underneath turn-up of the hem closely to the garment. This leaves the folded ½-inch section of the hem below the hemming line free to allow ease from lower hem edge to the shoulders. (Be sure the slip stitches do *not* prick through the outer lining.)

123

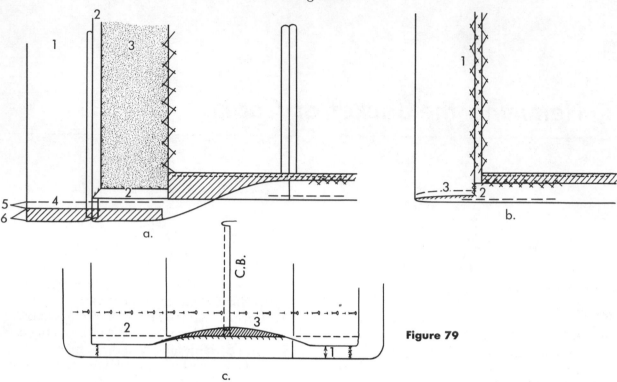

Figure 79

In the normal close-fitting sleeve, and in the sleeve with a vent at back seam, attach the lining to the sleeve in the same manner as the lower edge of the jacket.

In a garment with wide sleeves at the lower edge, the garment facing should be wider than 1½ inches. This will push the lining farther up into the sleeve so as not to be seen when the arm is raised. In a sleeve that is opened at the elbow seam for decorative purposes, the lining is not continuous at lower edge, but must be left open at elbow seam 1 inch higher than the sleeve opening. The lining edges parallel to the sleeve opening should be pushed far enough back from the open sleeve edge so that they do not show when worn. The lower edge of the lining is finished as in the normal sleeve.

Slip stitch the entire garment lining very closely to the garment, using stitches less than 1/16 of an inch apart.

If sunbak lining is used in a coat, it is wise to slip stitch the lining with buttonhole twist. Regular sewing silk is too light in weight to hold the heavy lining. (Sunbak is lining with a fleeced wool backing which is used instead of separate lining and interlining.)

HEMMING THE LONG COAT

Figure 80.

The hems of the long coat and lining are finished separately.

 a. The long coat is hemmed entirely across the hem and the facing. This will allow for alteration, if necessary. The hem may be finished as any of the hems illustrated in Fig. 35, pp. 70, 71.

 b. 1. The facing is then turned back onto the garment with the lower edge of the facing left open.

 2. The facing above hem is loosely catstitched to the hymo or to the garment itself if canvas is not used.

 3. The edge of the facing through the hem is closely catstitched to the hem, using ⅛-inch stitches.

BASTING THE GARMENT FACING INTO PLACE

Figure 81.

 a. 1. When the collar was joined to the garment it was basted into shape with edge basting and with diagonal basting on the collar surface. Leave these bastings in until the garment has its final steaming before inserting lining.

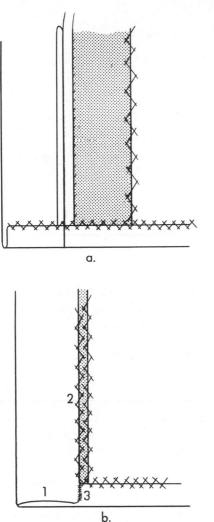

a.

b.

Figure 80

the opposite edge of facing onto the lapel edge earlier in the process of construction.

Pin the back edge of facing into place from neck, across shoulder, down side to bottom edge of garment.

Baste into position and catstitch to the canvas, and across to shoulder seam where it laps on top of shoulder pad.

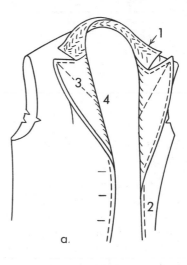

a.

2. Baste the facing around the edge from collar to lower edge of garment, rolling seam edge to the wrong side to the top button, where the seam is reversed and rolled to the opposite side of garment.
3. Beginning at the lapel point, baste diagonally from point to break line of lapel, rolling the lapel toward the coat as you baste.
4. With lapel uppermost, fold the facing back along break line and baste the facing loosely to garment along the break line, using diagonal bastings.
   b. Turn the garment over with lapel face down on the table.
   1. Place an ease thread along the facing opposite the break line. This will better allow for shrinking out any ease that might appear in facing, caused by easing

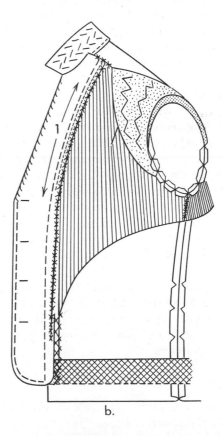

b.

Figure 81

Lining the Garment

LINING THE BODY OF THE GARMENT WITH SET-IN SLEEVES

The garment should be completely finished and steamed before the lining is put in. In fitting the lining fit the two sides in the same operation.

To insure the correct fit of the lining, the lining was earlier basted exactly the size of the garment after the garment was fitted. It should be stitched and pressed and ready for the garment.

Place the garment right side down on the table. Place the lining on the garment with wrong sides together and with underarm seams matching those of the garment. Pin the underarm seams of garment and lining together.

Frequently in fitting the garment the underarm has been lowered to increase the armscye.

The armscye of the lining should be checked against the garment before any permanent work is done. To do this, measure the armscye seam of the lining to the garment seam from the underarm seam up the front to shoulder, and up the back to the shoulder seam. There should be ample shoulder seam, at least ¾ inch, at both front and back of the lining to overlap at the shoulder.

Should there not be ample shoulder seams on the lining, raise the underarm seam of the lining along the garment seam. Clip the lining seam to fit the underarm of garment and to allow ample seam at shoulder.

Figure 82.

Match the underarm seams of lining and garment, and pin together.

a. Fold back the front lining from underarm seam and match the front edge of the underarm seams of lining to garment from armpit to bottom of garment. Stretch the garment seam slightly so that the lining will not be tight, and pin the two front edges of the two seams together.

These two seams are *permanently* basted together to within 3 inches of the hem edge. Repeat for second side. Fold the front lining sections into position on the garment.

b. 1. Match the front armscye of the lining to the garment from underarm up to the shoulder, and pin and baste into position to the armscye seam up to the shoulder pad; then pin to the shoulder pad up to the shoulder seam.

   The armscye seam of the garment is usually pressed wide open so that both front and back lining around the under half of the garment (between the ends of the shoulder pad), will fall across the garment seam edge. Baste to the sleeve seam, which is pressed into the sleeve.

2. If darts appear at the front shoulder, fold the marked dart of the lining into position, pin, and baste down to the width of chest, 4 to 5 inches below shoulder seam.

   Catstitch dart closely down the folded edge through the three thicknesses of the lining.

   Repeat for second side.

   With the garment flat on the table, smooth the front lining from underarm and armscye seams toward the front wool facing edge, keeping the cross and length grains straight with the garment grains.

126

3. Ease this section of the lining slightly onto the garment between underarm seams and front facings. This width ease prevents strain on both lining and garment. This is done by easing the lining onto the garment the full garment length and pinning into position with several rows of pins.

4. Turn the front edge of the lining under, allowing an overlap along the entire length of the back edge of the garment facing.

5. Turn back the surplus along this folded edge of the lining, pin, with pins at right angles to edge, and baste along the fold.

   Trim away any surplus material behind the folded edge, with cut edge parallel to folded edge.

6. Match the stitching lines of lining and garment across shoulder, pin, and baste into position using small diagonal basting or back stitch; fasten shoulder seam to garment and shoulder pad.

7. Match the lining on the edge of the garment facing from shoulder to lower edge of garment, pin, and baste into position. If there is to be a pocket in the lining, it should be inserted at this step in the lining of the garment, on the buttonhole side (see Fig. 67, pp. 108, 109 for pocket). Repeat (omitting pocket) for second lining front.

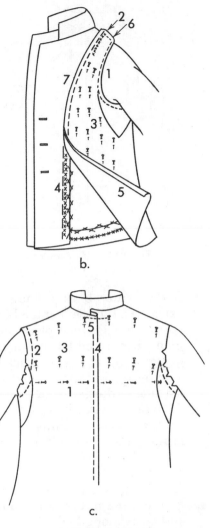

b.

c.

Figure 82 (Continued)

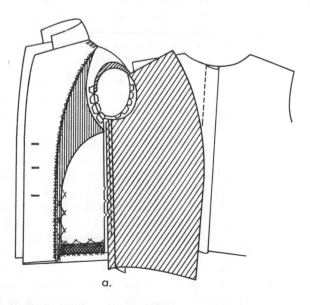

a.

Figure 82

c. With the back of the garment right side down on the table, take hold of the two lower back armscyes and pull lightly, bringing the grains of lining and garment into line.

1. Pin the lining closely to the garment with pins parallel to the floor. This keeps the upper section of the lining grain straight with garment back while fitting the upper lining into position.

2. Begin at underarm seam, match, pin, and baste armscye of lining to armscye of garment up the shoulder seam.

3. Smooth the lining up from the pinned section, 1, to neck and shoulder edges and pin into position, keeping center backs of lining and garment together.

   Repeat 2 and 3 for second side.

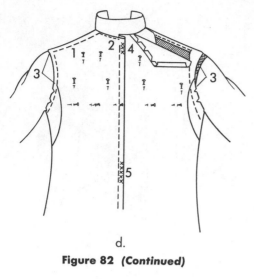

d.

Figure 82 *(Continued)*

4. If the center back fullness (the 3-inch extra width down center back which is basted in a 1½-inch pleat) needs adjustment, it may be let out or taken up to fit the width across the back.

5. The inside fold should be turned to the left side of the garment.

To prevent this inner fold of the center back pleat from falling loose inside the lining, hand stitch the pleat securely across the width at the neck edge just above the stitching line.

d. 1. Match the shoulder seams of lining to garment seam, turn to wrong side, pin, and baste along fold.

2. Clip the neck edge ⅛ inch, turn under lining until neck seams of lining and garment match, pin, and baste along fold. Repeat for second side.

Ease the basted shoulder and neck edges of the lining (1 and 2) into position across shoulder and neck, and pin into position.

3. To check the correct fit of the lining across the upper shoulders, grasp the upper back width of garment and lining and pull across width of back to determine whether there is strain. The lining should fit with ease, with no strain at any part of the back.

Should there be any strain, let out the center back pleat of the lining or rip the armscye lining from the garment and ease over onto the garment from the armscye seam.

4. The lining at neck is closely catstitched 1½ inches down through the three lining thicknesses along the pleat fold.

5. The lining at the waist may be held in place by catstitching along the pleat edge or across the pleat width. Sew the armscye seams together permanently, using a back stitch around the under armscye close to the armscye stitching edge on the garment, a loose stab stitch through the pad across the upper section of the armscye seam.

The entire lining is then closely slip stitched into position, using stitches less than ⅟₁₆ of an inch apart.

LINING THE SLEEVE

Figure 83.

When the length seams of the sleeves were fitted, the sleeve lining was basted to match exactly the garment sleeve size.

Stitch any darts and the length sleeve seams and steam.

a. 1. The seam at armscye is folded to the wrong side and an ease thread is placed along the exact fold, beginning and ending at the highest point of the sleeve.

2. Since the lining does not shrink, notch away the surplus ease of the seam on the inside of sleeve cap.

Match the correct sleeve lining to the correct garment sleeve. Turn the lining and the garment sleeves wrong side out.

b. 1. Match the stitching edge of the sleeve to the stitching edge of the garment seam at the underarm and pin into place.

2. From armscye to wrist, match the front sides of the underarm seams of lining and the garment and pin together. Stretch the garment sleeve slightly so that the lining will be slack along the seam.

Baste these two seams together permanently to within 3 inches of the folded edge at the wrist. Slip the hand through the sleeve lining at cap end; take hold of the lining and of garment at wrist and turn the lining right side out over the sleeve.

c. Match together any other armscye seams or darts of the lining to the garment, and pin together.

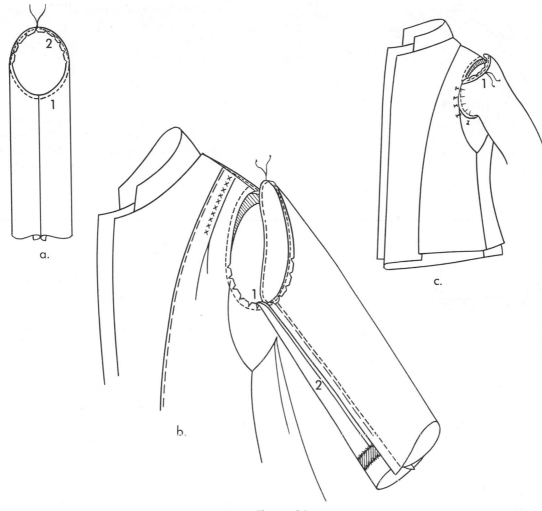

Figure 83

Pull up the ease thread at sleeve cap of lining, adjust the ease around the armscye edge of lining, and pin the entire lining armscye to the armscye of the garment, hiding the stitching line along the lining at armscye. Pin into place and baste.

Closely slip stitch the cap edge to garment lining.

LINING THE VENT AND THE BOTTOM OF THE LONG COAT

Figure 84.

If there is a vent in the coat at the back seam, attach the upper lining in the same manner as in a long coat, except for the center back ease (1½-inch-pleat) and around the vent at lower edge of lining.

a. The 3-inch ease at back was earlier basted in a 1½-inch pleat down center back. Place pins the length of garment on either side of pleat to hold the lining into place.

Place a basting down the edge fold at the center back of garment and release the pleat.

b. 1. Measure the vent overlap *in inches* on the garment being lined and baste from top to bottom edge of vent parallel to the folded edge.

2. Measure from the center back of the lining to the *right* the exact width of the vent width, *b*-1, and mark new fold edge. Transfer the center back pleat to the position marked to the right and baste the folded edge the full lining length.

3. The underneath folded edge *must* turn to the left on the inside of the lining.

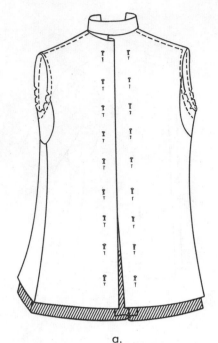

a.

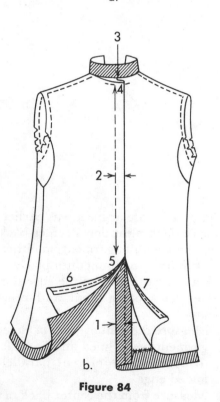

b.

Figure 84

tween these two points allowing the lining to fall slack.

Pin the lining into place at points 4 and 5 while working with the vent.

6. From the bottom of the lining, cut ¾ inch behind the basted fold up to the top of the vent.

7. Begin at 5 directly under the folded edge of the pleat, and fold back the lining from 5 to the lower garment edge exactly along the length grain and baste along the fold. Cut away the surplus material from vent top to lower hem edge, leaving ¾-inch seam.

Baste this folded edge of the lining, 7, to the inner edge of the vent width from the top of vent to hem edge.

When the vent opening edge, 6, is allowed to fall into place the two folded edges of the lining of the vent openings should fall together. Closely slip stitch vent edges (6 and 7) of lining to the garment.

This method of lining a vent leaves no outside cut at vent top to show on the lining side of the garment and is not easily torn from the garment as frequently occurs with vent linings.

The hem is handled the same as in a long coat.

HEMMING THE LINING OF THE LONG COAT

Figure 84c.

c. In the long coat, the hem of the garment and the hem of the lining are hemmed separately, so that the hem edge of the coat will not be pulled up by the lining, nor will the lining show below the hem edge.

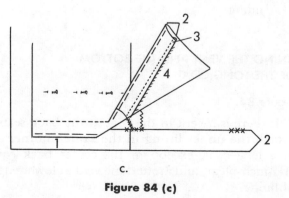

c.

Figure 84 (c)

4, 5. Baste the folded edge, 2, to the lining only from the neck edge to top opening of the vent.

To prevent the lining from being too short or too tight from the neck, 4, to the vent top, 5, pull the coat taut be-

Fasten the two hem edges together at the seams, and between seams if circumference of garment is wide, by ¾-inch long French tacks (see Fig. 87, p. 133). Release the 1½-inch pleat down the center back of the lining and leave free so that the lining hem edge is wider than garment hem across the back.

1. Measure the lining hem ¾ inch shorter than the garment, fold lining hem to wrong side, pin, and baste along fold.
2. Measure the lining hem the same width as garment hem, plus ⅜ inch for turn under.
3. Turn under the ⅜-inch allowance to the wrong side, baste, and machine stitch along folded edge. If the garment edge is flared at hem, folds will appear in the hem edge. Fold in where they fall naturally, before turning under ⅜ inch for edge stitching. Baste the open hem edge to the garment with seam edges matching.
4. Slip stitch the hem, placing stitches ¼ inch apart.

Remove all bastings and steam.

French tack the two hem edges together.

INTERLINING

Figure 85.

Interlining is handled as in the regular lining with a few exceptions.

a. When cutting the lining and interlining, smooth like pieces together with wrong sides facing; then pin and baste together as one piece. Baste as the regular lining and stitch the exact size of the garment.

b. 1. Down the front lining edge that fastens to the facing edge, cut back the interlining to the turn of the facing edge.
  2. Fold lining closely around this cut edge, baste, and catstitch to the interlining.

c. To hold the sleeve caps of lining and interlining together, machine stitch ¹⁄₁₆ inch toward the cap edge from the stitching armscye (2) edge before turning the seam to wrong side.

Place the ease thread around cap edge through four instead of two thicknesses of material as in the regular lining.

d. To lessen bulk at hem of a long coat, cut off the interlining at hem fold (1), turn the lining closely around the cut edge, and hand

hem to the lining so that the stitches do not show from the right side of the lining.

In the short jacket the hem at jacket and sleeve edges is handled as a single fabric.

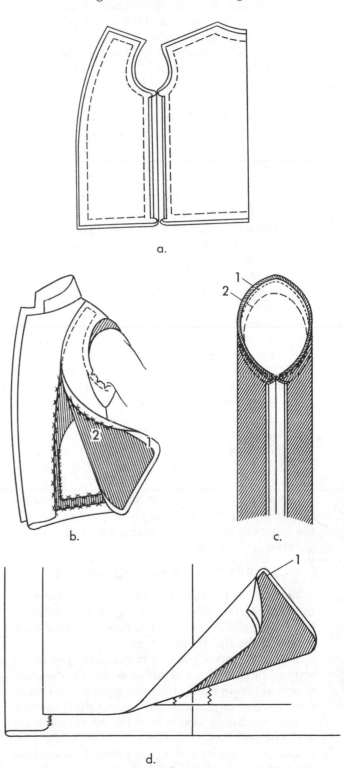

a.

b.

c.

d.

Figure 85

UNLINED GARMENT

Figure 86.

An unlined garment has seams and hems which must be finished, front canvas and shoulder pads which must be covered. The upper part of the garment will, therefore, have some lining.

Seams and hems may be bound with narrow bias binding (Fig. 35, pp. 70, 71), or the seams may be finished with machine zigzag and the hems bound.

To cover front canvas and shoulder pads, some lining must be used in the upper portion of the garment. This lining should be cut from the garment pattern, slightly longer than the canvas at lower edges.

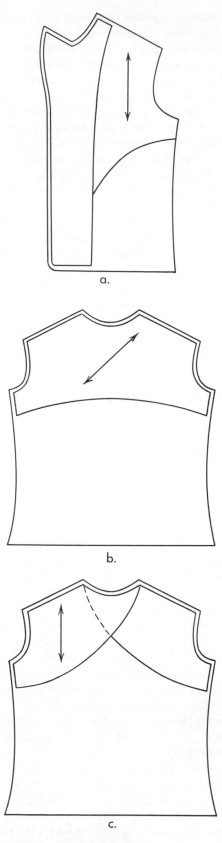

a.

b.

c.

Figure 86

   a. The front lining drops down from the shoulder and follows the front facing edge and armscye edge, and is cut down 3 inches below armscye curve to cover canvas used in the coat, also to conceal the armscye seam.

   b. The upper back may be cut in one piece from the back pattern, about 10 inches down at center back with back on the bias, curving down 3 inches below armscye to match the front lining.

   c. The back may be cut into two sections with the back on the straight grain. Cut from left neck edge, circling down below the right underarm; repeat for second side. This method prevents any strain across back between shoulders.

All lower raw edges of the lining must be finished.

Sleeves may or may not be lined. If not lined, the sleeve seam will need to be pressed toward the garment side so that seams and pads will be covered with the lining.

LINING THE RAGLAN OR KIMONO GARMENT

Sleeves in both the raglan and kimono garment must be sewed into the lining before lining is fitted into place. The 3-inch ease at center back is basted the full lining length.

Begin at center back of raglan and pin lining around neck edge to armscye seam. Fit the back seams of lining and garment together and baste from neck to underarm seam, using short stitches.

Slip the lining sleeve into the garment sleeve and pin and baste the two front seam edges together from underarm up to neck. This anchors the lining to the garment and prevents the lining from slipping out of place when worn.

The remainder of the lining is fitted like the garment with set-in sleeves.

In the raglan the lining is fastened along the shoulder seam and through the shoulder pad if a pad is used. The underarm sleeve seams are fastened together or, if a gusset is used, the two may be sewed together around the gusset seams.

FRENCH TACKS

Figure 87.

French tacks are used to hold two edges loosely together and may be any length desired.

    a. Using buttonhole twist, make three or four stitches connecting lining and garment hems opposite each other, having threads ¾ inch long.

    b. Buttonhole these threads around the full length of the loose threads. This allows freedom between the two garment sections and will prevent either garment edge from puckering.

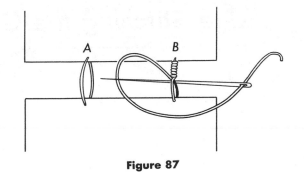

Figure 87

Edge Stitching the Garment

Figure 88.

Edge stitching is used to give a finished look to a tailored garment, and also to give a firm edge to fabrics which do not take a sharp press.

Hand stitching is a slow process, but the satisfaction one receives in the results is worth the effort.

Machine stitching is used more frequently than hand stitching and achieves the same results, except in appearance. However, it may be best to machine stitch some types of garments.

On all garments where there is an edge seam, the seam must be rolled slightly under to the wrong side so that the facing edge does not show from the right side. This edge should be basted carefully along the folded edge to hold it into position.

For edge stitching, place a guide basting, in addition to the edge basting, on the right side of the garment *exactly* parallel to the folded edge.

a. 1. Where a garment has a revere, reverse the right side of the garment at the point of the fold back at the top button position, or just below the shoulder seam if there is no collar.

All edge stitchings are done from the right side, so that the machine stitching *must* be ended at the reverse point, and started on opposite side of fabric. The stitching ends must touch and long threads from each stitching end must be left, threaded into a needle, pulled to the inside, and fastened invisibly. In this way the edge stitching will look continuous.

2. In a tailored coat, edge stitching may appear around the upper half of the sleeve, between widths of chest and back; patch pockets also may be edge stitched.

All edge stitching throughout the garment must be consistent in the width from the edge.

b, c. If a garment has a notched lapel, the stitching lines should be shaped at the point where collar and lapel join. In hand stitching, one of three methods may be used (*d, e, f*). Matching buttonhole twist is used.

d. Hand stitching is made by stab stitching, one stitch at a time. Push the needle straight through to the wrong side, pull the thread through, return the needle straight through to the right side and pull the thread through. One stitch is completed at a time, the stitches being the same length on each side of the garment.

e. The needle is pushed diagonally through the fabric, the thread pulled through; then the needle is returned diagonally to right side, making a very tiny prick stitch on each side of the garment.

f. The needle is pushed diagonally through to wrong side and thread is pulled through; a back stitch is taken and the needle is pushed diagonally through to right side.

This back stitch is used only for a very spongy or bulky fabric where neither stitch will hold the fabrics firmly together.

In appearance on the surface, this stitch may have a prick stitch or stitch $\frac{1}{8}$ inch in length.

134

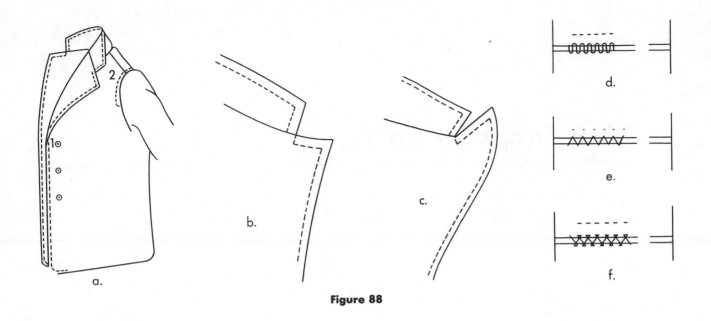

Figure 88

Arm Straps for Coats

Figure 89.

Arm straps are used to hold a coat into position when worn as a cape.

The straps may be made of the fabric of the coat or of the lining, approximately 9 to 12 inches long, 1 to 1½ inches wide when finished.

    a. Either one may be sewed flat to the garment if made of the wool or to the lining if made from lining fabric.

    b. Either one may be sewed to the fabric or to the lining, forming a loop which falls flat against the garment when worn as a coat.

To make the straps, cut the fabric lengthwise, twice the desired width and the length, plus ⅜-inch seam all the way around.

Stitch across end and along the side until one inch to the center. Repeat for second end and side. Clip across the two stitched corners to within ¹⁄₁₆ inch to the stitching turn, and steam the seams wide open.

Turn the two ends right side out through the 2-inch opening along the side. Baste the entire strap around the seam area and slip stitch the 2-inch open seam. Steam, remove basting, and resteam.

Place these straps with the top end approximately 9 to 11 inches down from the shoulder seam. Slip stitch each end securely to the garment.

When the garment is worn around the shoulders as a cape the arms are slipped through these straps to hold the coat on the shoulders. The straps may be pushed up over the shoulders and the coat may be carried on the back instead of over the arm.

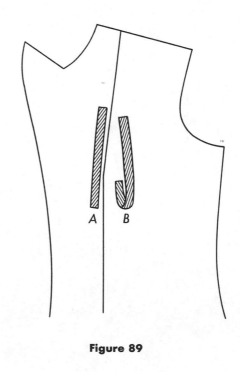

Figure 89

136

Slacks

Figure 90.

Making a pair of slacks is not very different from making a skirt. The measurements and fittings are similar except through the crotch.

Slacks may have side front pleats or may be fitted smoothly with darts both front and back, depending on fashion and one's preference.

 a. The crotch should be fitted close enough to look well when standing, but loose enough for comfort when bending or sitting.

   The side seams should hang perpendicular to the floor and the ease through the hips and legs should be ample for comfort at all times.

   1. Crotch measurement may be taken in either of two ways. Pin a tape tightly around the waist from which the measurement is taken. Seat a person on a flat-surfaced chair with space at the side, or upon a table. The measurement is taken from the normal waistline to chair seat along side seam and perpendicular to floor. Double this measurement for entire crotch and add 2 inches or more for ease.

   2. The crotch may be measured from the center front waist, through the crotch around to the center back waist line, plus two inches or more for ease.

     In either measurement taken, some persons may desire slightly more ease.

If slacks do not have a belt, the waist line will be raised above the normal waist line, but this added height *must not* be counted in the crotch measurement.

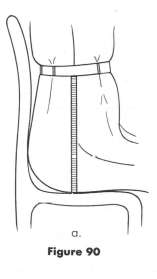

a.

Figure 90

 b. Measurement of the figure with minimum allowance for ease.

   1. Waistline: snug enough to stay in place.
   2. Hip: 3 inches down, plus 1-inch ease or more.
   3. Hip: 6 inches down, plus 2-inch ease or more.
   4. Widest hip of the figure, plus 2–4 inches for ease.
   5. Crotch, plus 2 inches for ease or more.
   6. Along side seam for leg length.

Selection of pattern is important if one wishes to make few alterations. Whether the hips are wide or narrow, whether waist small or large, select a pattern that better fits the hips; for the hip alteration is more difficult than that of the waist.

 c. Measure the pattern.
   Pin out all darts or pleats in pattern.
   Pencil in all seam allowances at center front, center back, if printed patterns are not used.

137

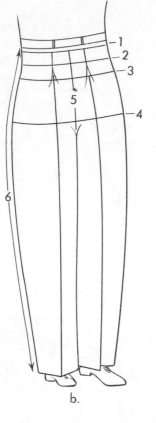

b.

Figure 90 (Continued)

Check all pattern measurements against the figure measurements and mark needed alterations on the pattern.

e. Pattern alteration.

1. To increase crotch length cut across pattern halfway between waist line and crotch. Pin new tissue under cut edges and spread the pattern the amount needed.

2. Repeat lengthening of the leg in the same manner, halfway between crotch and hem edge.

   Repeat for back pattern and check length grain with ruler to keep the grain length in line.

3, 4. To decrease crotch or leg length, fold in a tuck at the same positions as in 1 and 2, removing from the pattern the excess length.

   Recheck grain lengths of pattern, crotch length, and leg length after the above alterations.

5. If pattern is too tight through the hips, cut both front and back patterns from the waist to within ¼ inch of bottom of

Waist and crotch seams.

Turn up hem at bottom of leg.

Pin pattern pieces together along side seams to the position opposite the crotch.

Check measurements 1–6 against figure measurements, and plan both the position and amount of each alteration needed. (All measurements are to be taken between seams or between seam and hem allowance.)

1. Waist line.
2. 3-inch hip.
3. 6-inch hip.
4. Widest hip.
5. Crotch front and back.
6. Leg length along side seam.

d. To check the accuracy of length grain, fold slacks with inside leg seam below crotch flush with side leg seam.

   Crease the folded edge formed at center of leg pattern, which should give the accurate grain length. Repeat for back leg pattern. Rule along the entire crease so as not to lose the grain length.

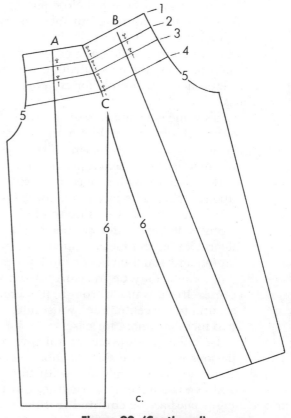

c.

Figure 90 (Continued)

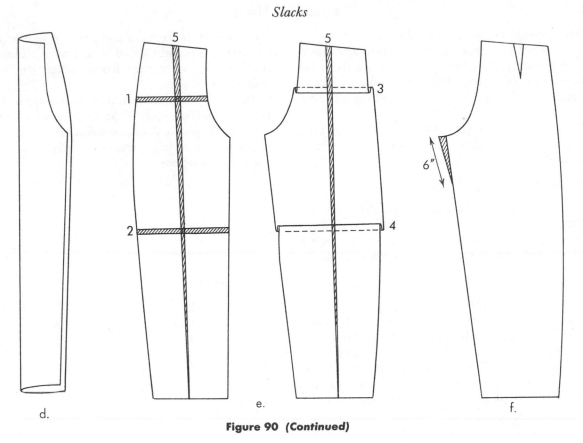

Figure 90 (Continued)

leg along the length grain and spread each pattern ¼ the desired circumference increase.

Pin tissue under spread.

Redraw a new grain length on each pattern piece as in *d*.

f. Some figures have very full hips at back and may need extra crotch length. This may be added by extending the back crotch up to 1 inch and extending the increase 6 inches down the leg (or 1½ inches 8 inches down leg).

To cut slacks:

Place folded fabric on table with torn edge parallel to table end, and selvage edge parallel to side of table.

Place pattern on fabric with length grain parallel to selvage, and pin into place.

If stripes are used, they must match one on top of another in the fabric before cutting.

If plaids are used the plaid must be matched in both the length and cross grains of the fabric when folded, and must match around the figure when cut. Cut pocket section matching in both **grain and design.**

If a belt is used, cut on the length grain, twice the desired width plus seams and the length needed plus overlap and seams.

Mark all stitching lines and placket edges with chalk, transfer paper or tailor tacks.

Along the left side placket opening where the zipper will be placed, mark 3 inches out from stitching edge for facing the zipper on the back edge and for facing the pocket on the front edge. These extensions will eliminate sewing extra material for finishing the zipper opening.

To baste slacks:

Baste in all waistline darts the length indicated on pattern, or front pleats 3½ inches down if pleats appear at side front.

Place basting along matching placket edges at left side of slacks.

Place basting along pocket edges on right side of slacks.

Baste center front seams together through the crotch.

Baste center back seams together through the crotch.

Baste side seams together. On the left side baste from lower edge of placket to hem edge.

Baste inside leg seams together.

Turn waist line seam to wrong side and baste.

Cut a facing 2 inches wide or more from the folded edge of a true bias of silesia or heavy sateen. Turn down a ½-inch seam along cut edge and baste.

If a belt is used turn down seam allowance along each edge, baste and steam, remove bastings, and resteam.

To fit slacks:

(See fitting of skirt, Fig. 29, pp. 64, 65.)

Pin bias around waist with seam to outside at upper edge and opening at left side. If a belt is used pin around waist with open seam at lower edge.

Slip on slacks and pin up placket on left side and pocket opening on right side.

Pin center front, center back, and side seams to waistline band, with top edges of slacks and band matching, or pin slacks to lower belt edge.

Begin at center front and pin slacks to facing, slightly easing slacks onto band for ease over hip curves. Pin across to side seams. Repeat for back.

If hips are large and waist small, it may be necessary to fit out excess fullness at waistline, at the darts, the front pleats, at the center front and back seams, or down side seams.

If the slacks are too large through the hips, fit out the excess ease at the two side seams at the leg length.

If the crotch is too loose, lift the slacks all the way around on the waistline facing and take off surplus across the top of the waistline.

If the crotch is too tight, narrow the waistline facing to allow the slacks to drop slightly lower around the waistline.

g. 1, 2. If diagonal wrinkles appear at seat in back of slacks, raise the slacks across the back waist and repin to the belt.

Fit out excess fullness down back crotch seam, and along back leg seam 6 inches below crotch. This should remove wrinkles and allow side seam to hang perpendicular to the floor.

3, 4. If wrinkles appear across stomach at front, raise the front across waist line and pin into position. Fit out excess fullness down front crotch seam, and along leg seam 6 inches below crotch. This should remove wrinkles and allow side seam to hang perpendicular to the floor.

Carefully tailor tack top edge of slacks to belt or facing, placing tacks 1 inch apart. Mark position on belt at center front, center back, and side seam.

Baste across each matching belt end, and separate slacks from belt so as to be able to rebaste all fittings; stitch darts, pleats, crotch, and inside leg seams, making garment ready to set in the pocket and zipper.

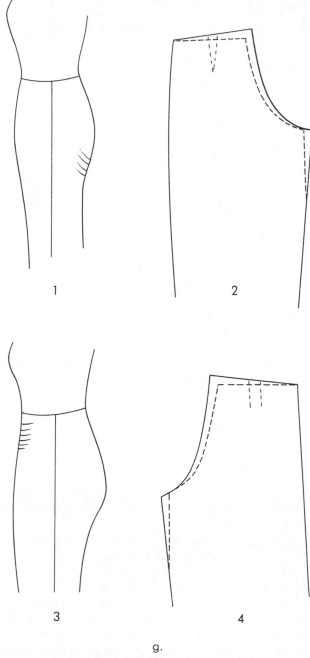

1   2

3   4

g.

Figure 90 (Continued)

POCKETS

Slacks may have pockets on both sides in seam and placket, or in the right side seam only, or pockets may be made 2 inches in front of and parallel to side seam. This last mentioned pocket is made in the same manner as a corded pocket in a suit or coat (Fig. 61, pp. 100, 101) and is 5 to 5½ inches long at opening when finished. The bag of silesia is the same size from top edge of pocket as a pocket in a seam.

If slacks are made of cotton, the pockets will be made from the same material and will not need the strips of fabric along pocket edges.

In wool, the bag is made of silesia or similar material so will need to be faced along the pocket sides to prevent the silesia from showing at the pocket opening.

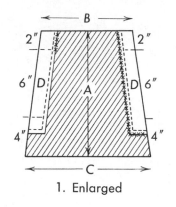

1. Enlarged

Figure 91.

a. Pocket in the right-hand side slack seam.
  1. Pocket bag may be made of silesia or of sateen.
     a. 13 inches long with center on length grain.
     b. 10 inches across top.
     c. 12 inches across bottom.
     d. Wool facing 10 inches by 3 inches.
     Place wool facings on the bag edge, baste outer edge, and stitch inner edge to silesia. Either catstitch or machine zigzag stitch over stitched edge to prevent fraying.
     On each wool edge of pocket mark down 2 inches from narrow top edge; then mark off 6 inches below that for pocket opening. The remaining 4 inches will form the bag below pocket opening. The top of this bag will begin at the normal waist line and *not* extend to top edge of slacks where the waist extends above the normal waist.
  2. Side seams of the slacks have been fitted and rebasted.
     Mark with basting the normal waistline in both 2 and 3.
     Mark with basting the position of the pocket on both front and back of side seam and open up the seam about 12 inches down to make the pocket.
     On the two matching seam edges of right side of the slacks mark 2 inches down from normal waistline basting, then 6 inches below that for pocket opening.

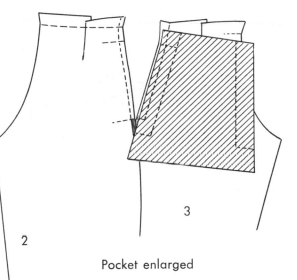

Pocket enlarged

Figure 91 (a)

  3. Match the pocket bag to the stitching line of side seams of the front slacks with right sides together, baste and stitch along the marked 6-inch pocket opening. Repeat for the back edge of side seam.
     Steam press seams wide open.
  4. Rebaste and stitch the side seam above the pocket to top of slacks, matching the stitching end to the pocket stitching.
     At the lower edge of pocket opening, clip the seam of the pocket to the stitching end and fold pocket bag away from the leg seam. Baste and stitch the leg seam from lower pocket opening to bottom of slacks.
     Steam leg seams wide open.
  5. From the right side, fold the pocket flat against the front of the leg, and baste the seam edge along the pocket opening.
     Machine stitch ⅜ or ½ inch along opening of the pocket length.

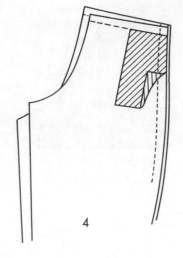

4

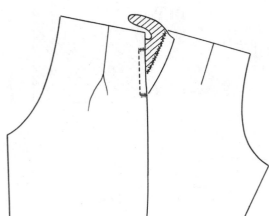

5

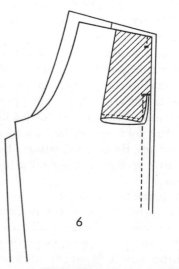

6

Figure 91 (a) (Continued)

6. From the wrong side baste and stitch the bag from lower pocket bag to the lower pocket edge, then across bottom to the folded edge, stitching back on each stitching end to prevent ripping.

From the right side make a bar from stitching end to seam edge at each end of the pocket, as shown in 5. These stitches should be stab stitched through the pocket to prevent ripping. (See Fig. 68d, p. 110.)

Sew the upper width of the pocket bag to the lower edge of belting.

b. In many slacks the zipper is placed in the pocket bag itself, two inches in from the stitching edge of the pocket where it joins the back edge of the side seam. This prevents the zipper from showing along the placket opening.

Cut the bag with the center on the length grain.

    14 inches long
    11 inches across at top
    13 inches across the bottom

Cut two wool facings

    10 inches long by 4 inches wide
    10 inches long by 2 inches wide

1. Place basting 9 inches down from top and 2½ inches in from right-hand side for zipper position.

2. Place the 4-inch wool strip over zipper position with right side of wool facing wrong side of pocket, and baste into position.

From right side stitch a rectangle around the basting, stitching ⅛ inch from basting.

3. Cut along basting to within 3⁄16 inch of end, then diagonally out to corner turns. Turn wool to right side of the garment, baste around stitched edge, and steam.

4. On left-hand edge baste the 2-inch strip. Stitch along inside edge and across bottom of each strip; then catstitch over raw edge or use machine zigzag stitch.

Begin at the bottom, pin, baste, and stitch an 8-inch zipper into the pocket.

5. *a.* With right sides facing, pin, baste, and stitch the pocket into the left side seam of the slacks.

Stitch down 9 inches from the top edge, which will end the stitching opposite the zipper end.

b. At top front edge stitch pocket and slacks the width of 2 inches across the top to finish for buttonhole overlap.

6. *a.* Stitch the side leg seam below the placket end, matching stitching ends of placket, and steam.

b. At the front or overlap of pocket, turn the pocket to the inside, slightly roll the seam to wrong side, baste, and stitch ⅜ inch along open edge of placket.

c. From the back placket edge, press the pocket straight out from the stitching edge.

Stitch the bag from lower placket edge down to turn and across bottom, as in Pocket i–6. Join belting to top of slacks as in Fig. 28, pp. 63, 64.

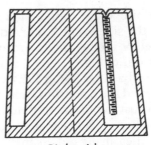

4. Right side

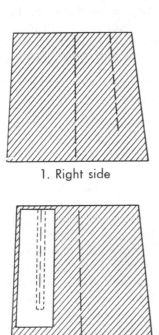

1. Right side

2. Wrong side

3. Wrong side

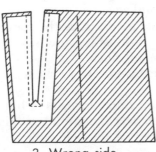

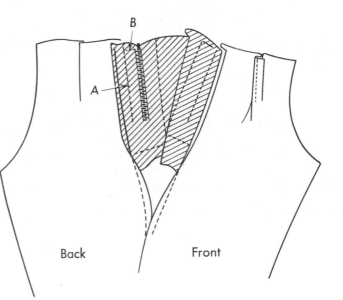

5. Wrong side

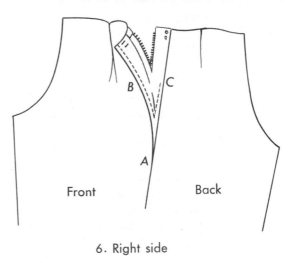

6. Right side

Figure 91 (b)

c. Pocket in the left or zipper side of slacks.

1. Baste the side seam from bottom edge of placket, 9 inches down from waistline, to bottom of leg.

   Place bastings along the two matching placket edges, a continuation of side seam from waist to bottom of placket.

2. On the back placket edge make an underlap by measuring out ³⁄₁₆ inch from basted placket edge, fold under, and baste along folded edge. Steam edge, remove basting, and resteam to remove basting imprint.

   This edge will receive the zipper.

3. The pocket bag of silesia or sateen is cut the same size as the bag for the right side in pocket *a*.

   On the right-hand edge of the pocket, baste a 3-inch wool facing, stitch inner edge to silesia then catstitch or zigzag by machine to prevent fraying.

4. *a*. The front edge or overlap of placket has been cut with an extension of 3 inches out from the matching placket edge.

   b. Place the left-hand edge of pocket along the basted placket edge, allowing the 3-inch extension to fall over on the pocket bag. Baste into position, stitch along wool edge, and catstitch or use machine zigzag over raw edge.

   c. On the opposite edge, fold the edge of the pocket bag to the wrong side and baste.

   d. Two inches down from the top of the pocket, baste and stitch the front edge of a 6-inch zipper.

5. *a*. Fold the pocket bag to wrong side along the matching placket edge and baste.

   b. Stitch the leg seam from zipper end to leg bottom, matching the pocket and leg stitchings at end of pocket.

   c. Beginning 3 inches down from the waistline, stitch ¼ or ⅜ inch back from the folded edge, which will be the pocket opening.

   d. Baste and sew the back edge of the zipper to the side seam of the leg. Start from the bottom and work up so that the zipper works smoothly when closed.

   e. A 3-inch wide fabric extension cut on the length grain may be placed behind

and stitched on with the zipper to prevent zipper from catching into undergarments.

6. Close the zipper and turn garment to wrong side. Stitch bag from end of pocket opening down the side and across the bottom.

   If a belt is used, start the top edge of zipper and pocket at the belt edge. Attach the top edge of the pocket to the lower belt edge.

   If a facing is used on inside waistline, fasten the top of pocket bag to the lower facing edge.

7. Make a bar tack at each end of pocket opening from stitching to pocket edge. These stitches are stab stitched through the pocket to prevent ripping.

   Make two buttonholes on the overlap with buttons on the underlap.

   If a pocket is not made on the left or zipper side, finish the placket in the same manner as one on a skirt (see Fig. 32, pp. 67, 68).

FINISHING WAISTLINE OF SLACKS

The slacks were earlier fitted to the bias facing or belt, tailor tacked, and separated to finish the upper portion.

With right side stitching edges together match the tacked facing to the tacked waistline and ends at placket opening. Baste into position and stitch along seam edge. Steam seam open; then roll and baste the facing to the wrong side.

Fasten the facing to all seams and darts, but do not allow stitches to appear on right side.

If desired, stitching may be used across the top waistline edge ½ or ³⁄₁₆ inch down from edge.

Belt guards are used on faced slacks to hold the belt into position. Cut strips of fabric 1 inch wide and of the length desired, plus ¼ inch at each end for seams, for as many belt guards as needed. Stitch in a tube along the length, turn to right side, and steam.

Place guards at darts, both front and back, side seam at right side, and just behind the placket on the left side.

Turn end seams in toward the loop to conceal stitching.

Sew invisibly into place, and buttonhole or closely catstitch over the raw edges. Place the top of guard ¼ to ½ inch below the top edge of waistline.

If a belt is used instead of a facing, it is attached at the top in the same manner as that of a skirt (see Fig. 28, pp. 63, 64).

The top width of the pocket is stitched to the lower edge of the facing. If a belt is used, it is stitched with the top of slacks into the lower edge of the belt.

CUFFS ON SLACKS

Figure 92.

1. Mark slack length. The slacks should not break over the instep and should hang about ¼ inch longer at the back over the heel. Turn the hem to the right side of leg along the marked length and baste along folded edge.
2. Release seam of the turned-up section until the cut edge fits smoothly around leg width.
3. Mark up from folded edge 1½ to 1¾ inches on the turned-up section, mark for the cuff width, and place basting.
4. Fold hem section down to right side along marked cuff edge and baste along top edge of cuff.
5. Fold surplus hem around the slack length up into the leg and baste along fold at bottom edge of trousers. Check cuff width for accuracy, 1¼ or 1¾ inches.
6. Turn leg wrong side out. Measure from bottom edge 1¼ inch for hem width, mark, and trim away the surplus hem. Baste hem edge to trousers but not through the cuff.
7. Catstitch hem edge to the trouser leg, using ¼-inch stitches.
8. Tack the inside seam edge of cuff to the leg seam, ⅜ inch down from the fold of the cuff. Steam cuff, remove all bastings, resteam to remove basting marks. Steam front and back length leg crease through cuff.

PLAIN HEM AT BOTTOM OF SLACKS

Figure 93.

Mark leg length, turn hem to wrong side, and baste along folded edge.

Turn leg wrong side out, measure up 1½ inches from folded edge, mark, and trim away the surplus. Closely catstitch the hem to the leg. Remove all bastings, steam the hem, then steam the length front and back crease through the hem.

1

2

3

Figure 91 (c)

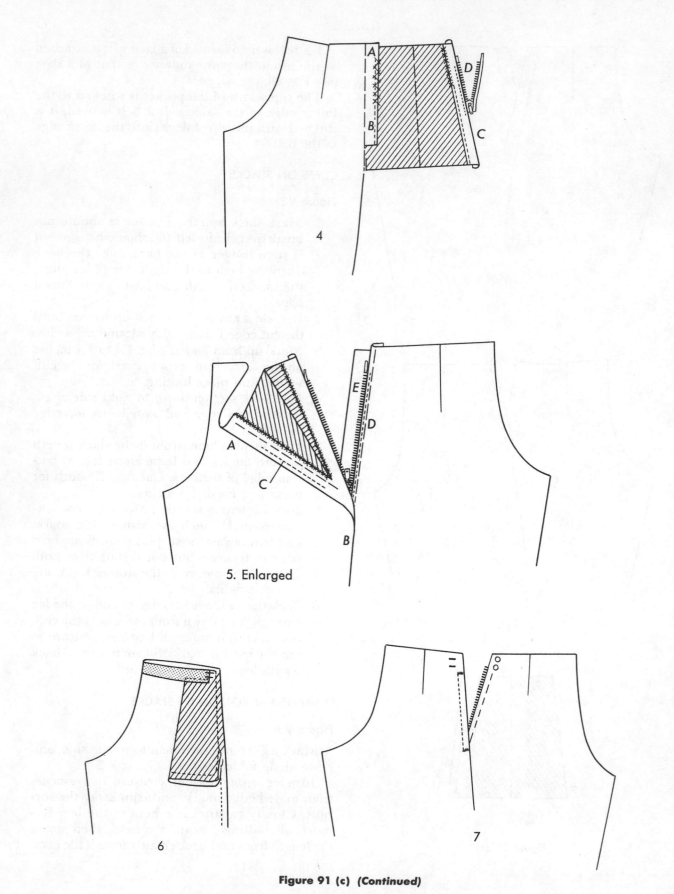

4

5. Enlarged

6

7

Figure 91 (c) (Continued)

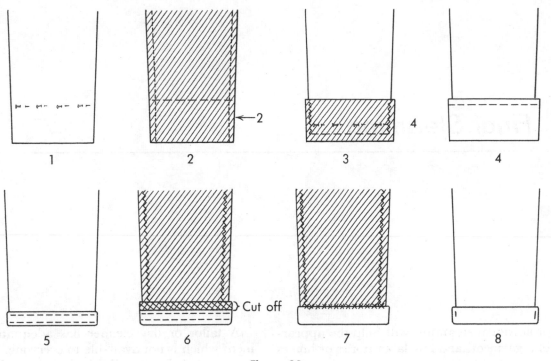

Figure 92

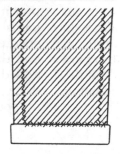

Figure 93

Final Steaming

A professional steaming will help the appearance of a garment, and few laboratories or homes have equipment for this steaming.

During the process of construction each garment part is steamed, following the steaming suggestions given on page 5. However this is not enough for all materials. Some spongy fabrics do not take a sharp edge and are difficult to steam. Closely woven hard twisted yarns in fabrics are apt to become shiny when steamed and fabrics with a heavy nap or pile may be flattened out in some areas of the garment.

A tailor or dry cleaner has adequate equipment which is not available to everyone. It is recommended that the finished garment be taken for a final steaming to be done by a tailor or dry cleaner. However, the operator should be warned that it is a newly made garment and that great pains should be taken when steaming. These operators have been found to be most co-operative and the appearance achieved is well worth the added cost. In fact this final steaming improves some garments to such an extent that it covers up poor workmanship.